Praise for Jim Donovan

"*Handbook to a Happier Life* is great! It is brief, easy to read, practical, and filled with useful exercises for making positive changes. This little book should be a part of everyone's self-help library."

— Jack Canfield, coauthor of *Chicken Soup for the Soul*

"Jim Donovan's *Handbook to a Happier Life* is delicious and delightful! Jim has taken the best 'ingredients' of life and shown us how we can combine them into just the recipe we need to help us create a fulfilling life."

— Wally Amos, author of *The Cook Never Crumbles*

"How often do you hear really good ideas time after time and fail to act on them? Then, that same idea comes to you one more time, and that time you act on it, and you wonder what took you so long. What was it about Donovan's life planning book that enabled me to do what I've failed at many other times? Perhaps it's the read, think, and write format. These thoughtful exercises are all about you and where you want to go."

— Barbara Garro, writer, *Business Talk*

"I've read many self-help and self-improvement books but *Handbook to a Happier Life* is simply the best."

— John Kiple, business executive

"A delight! First-rate, proven concepts, supported with personal experiences and presented in bite-size chunks that anyone can use."

— Emmet Robinson, author of
How to Prosper in Business, Regardless of the Economy

D0096809

happy@work

Also by Jim Donovan

Handbook to a Happier Life (New World Library, 2003)

Take Charge of Your Destiny (Austin Bay, 2005)

Stop Living Paycheck to Paycheck (Austin Bay, 2008)

Don't Let an Old Person Move into Your Body (Austin Bay, 2010)

52 Ways to a Happier Life (Tremendous Life Books, 2011)

What Are You Waiting For? It's Your Life (Sound Wisdom, 2013)

happy@work

60 Simple Ways to Stay Engaged and Be Successful

Jim Donovan

Foreword by Steve Rizzo

New World Library
Novato, California

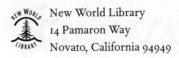 New World Library
14 Pamaron Way
Novato, California 94949

Copyright © 2014 by Jim Donovan

All rights reserved. This book may not be reproduced in whole or in part, stored in a retrieval system, or transmitted in any form or by any means — electronic, mechanical, or other — without written permission from the publisher, except by a reviewer, who may quote brief passages in a review.

Text design by Tona Pearce Myers

Library of Congress Cataloging-in-Publication Data
Donovan, Jim, [date].
Happy at work : 60 simple ways to stay engaged and be successful / Jim Donovan.
    pages   cm
ISBN 978-1-60868-250-8 (pbk. : alk. paper) — ISBN 978-1-60868-251-5 (ebook)
1. Job satisfaction. 2. Quality of work life. I. Title.
HF5549.5.J63D66 2014
650.1—dc23   2013045132

First printing, April 2014
ISBN 978-1-60868-250-8
Printed in the USA on 100% postconsumer-waste recycled paper

 New World Library is proud to be a Gold Certified Environmentally Responsible Publisher. Publisher certification awarded by Green Press Initiative. www.greenpressinitiative.org

10 9 8 7 6 5 4 3 2 1

50.1 DON
748 1188 9/9/14   WBL
onovan, Jim, 1946 June 11-

appy @ work
     ABJ

For God and the angels,
who have watched over and protected me
and are the inspiration for everything I write

LeRoy Collins Leon County
Public Library System
200 West Park Avenue
Tallahassee, FL 32301

Contents

Acknowledgments

I want to especially acknowledge the two Georgias in my life. First I'd like to thank my wife, Georgia, who has supported my writing from the very beginning and who has been by my side through it all. In addition to her support, her knowledge and experience in the upper levels of corporate management have been my sanity check throughout the writing of this book.

Georgia Hughes, editorial director at New World Library (NWL), has been my friend and champion since my first book and has made it possible for me to be published by NWL. Words cannot express the gratitude and appreciation I have for her continued support.

I'd also like to thank:

Marc Allen, publisher at NWL and one of the most honorable and supportive people in publishing. His willingness to publish *Handbook to a Happier Life* began what is now a ten-year relationship between us. Thank you, Marc.

Of course, all the amazing staff at New World Library. You are a class act.

Art director Tracy Cunningham and production director Tona Pearce Myers: Thank you for this fantastic cover and overall design. I am proud to have my name on such a great-looking book.

Managing editor Kristen Cashman, copy editor Mimi Kusch, and assistant editor Jonathan Wichmann: It's great having such a great team. Many thanks.

Publicists Monique Muhlenkamp and Kim Corbin: Without you, no one would know about this book. I am so appreciative of being able to work with you.

My longtime friend and mastermind partner Art (Ski) Swiatkowski for helping me stay on track, holding me accountable, and, most of all, being my friend and living the dream.

Foreword

W hat's your definition of success? Does it simply mean making a lot of money? Perhaps to you success means achieving a goal at any cost.

Here's my point, dear reader: Let's say your goal is to become a vice president of a big company. After many years of intense stress, worry, and an avalanche of emotional, mental, and physical overload, you finally achieve your goal, along with all the wealth and prestige that come with it. Is this success? If you consult a dictionary, the answer would be yes. Webster's Dictionary defines successes as follows: "1. The favorable or prosperous termination of attempts or endeavors. 2. The attainment of wealth, position, honors, or the like." I think it's amazing that the word *happy* or *happiness* is not included in the definition of the word *success*. Unfortunately, our conventional definition of success is simply achieving the goal. Not enough emphasis is placed on the value of experiencing the journey, building character, and learning life lessons along the way.

The truth is, it really doesn't matter how much money you have, or how famous you are, or how many goals you've achieved. It makes no difference how big your house is or what industry accolades you've racked up in your career. The entire world can view your life as the ultimate success story, but the bottom line is this: if you are not happy, you are not successful! If you are not enjoying yourself on your journey toward your goal, you're ripping yourself off. Trust me. There are enough people willing to do that for you.

That is why I love this book! *Happy@Work* reminds us that *success* and *happiness* are synonymous, but only if you choose to live your life accordingly. Jim Donovan reveals valuable intangibles that most people don't consider as important criteria of leading a happy and successful life, both professionally and personally.

Whether you are in sales, service, education, health care, or any other business, this book is written for you. It's a wake-up call that makes you realize that life is based on the choices you make. You are the master of your destiny. And you can succeed — while enjoying the process — regardless of your circumstances.

Why should you read this book and buy a copy for someone you know? Because it's filled with wonderful, out-of-the-box ideas and strategies that will take you to a better place not only in business but in life. In my view, that's the ultimate success.

— Steve Rizzo,
author of *Get Your SHIFT Together*

Introduction

I n recent years numerous studies have been conducted about happiness and fulfillment in the workplace. Unfortunately, most of them report dismal numbers when it comes to employee happiness.

A 2012 Gallup poll reported employee disengagement in US companies to be as high as 70 percent, costing businesses more than $550 billion a year in lost productivity.

While I'm not claiming to have any magic-bullet solution to this appalling situation, I have learned powerful methods for becoming more engaged, fulfilled, and productive both at work and in my personal life. I take pride in the fact that everything I write is based on my own experience. It's not theory. I have walked the walk and continue to use these principles daily in my own life.

I wrote *Happy@Work* to provide you with simple, easy-to-implement ideas that you can use to move toward creating an amazing career — and life. You have the right to enjoy everything in your life, especially your work; however, doing so requires you to take ownership of your circumstances, define what you want, and act in alignment with the laws of the Universe.

Each chapter is designed to stand on its own, containing a single idea that you can apply to and integrate into your life. If you're constantly rushing out the door trying not to be late for work, the chapters about changing your habits and the one about arriving early may be where you want to start reading.

Some of the most important chapters regarding your career are the ones that explore your dreams and desires, helping you to create a compelling vision and to set and achieve your goals. One of the biggest reasons so many people feel disconnected from their work is that they haven't learned to explore why they do what they do and what it means to them.

Several chapters are devoted to helping you manage your physical energy and to feeling better, as well as suggestions and exercises to help you take charge of your emotions. Others include suggestions on how to manage difficult people and stressful situations. Do you find yourself working harder and harder but accomplishing less and less? Then be sure to read chapter 11, on taking inspired action.

Many chapters in *Happy @ Work* end with Activity Steps. These consist of simple questions to ask yourself or suggestions to consider. Completing these steps is crucial to your success. While simply reading this book will provide you with ideas and information, it is the self-discovery you gain by answering the questions and completing the exercises that will create lasting change and lead you toward the life you desire.

As with all my books, I suggest you evaluate the information here as it pertains to your own life. You are the master of your destiny, the architect of your life, and it is vital that whatever ideas you adapt to your life resonate with you and are appropriate. Take from this book what works for you, and leave the rest.

I believe that each of us knows what's best for our life and, in the end, that is our responsibility. There are already too many people preaching dogma. I'm not going to be one of them.

Other Ways to Use This Book

Use this book as a tool — an idea generator, if you will. You may want to read it from beginning to end, chapter by chapter, or you may want to jump around, reading those chapters that can help you with a present challenge or situation, as mentioned above. If you're time pressed in the morning just take a moment and read a single chapter. Doing so will give you a thought for the day and start your day off on a positive note.

Here's another way you can use this book in your day-to-day life: while thinking about a particular situation or challenge, just open to a random page and read the lesson it contains. Believe it or not, I sometimes do this with my own books. I think you'll be pleasantly surprised by how often you gain a new insight from doing this.

If you're a manager or team leader you may want to choose one or two of the chapter topics to use as a meeting starter and build a discussion around it. Simply have your team members read the chapter either before or at the start of the meeting. If the chapter includes Activity Steps, you can then use those as conversation starters. You may even want to buy copies for your salespeople to give as a gift to prospective customers as a way to warm up cold calls and initial meetings.

The way you use this book is, of course, up to you.

I wish you the very best in your life and career. If, at any time, I can be of service to you or your company, please contact me.

happy@work

1. *Reward Yourself and Others*

Have you ever noticed how easily we criticize ourselves and others for making even the most minor mistakes? Most of us have no problem finding fault, especially with ourselves. In many cases, unfortunately, managers see criticism as a way to embarrasses people into performing better.

Verbally berating someone and expecting her to perform better is like hitting your computer with a hammer and expecting it to run better. It doesn't work. I doubt that it ever did, but it certainly does not work with today's more skilled workforce. And if you do this with the Millennial Generation, you'll soon see your workforce walking out the door.

Managing by bossing people around was a popular practice back in the Industrial Age; however, we've learned over time that there are much more effective ways to manage people.

If you must criticize an employee's performance, be sure to do it in private. Correcting someone's behavior publicly not only can cause the person in question to suffer but can also have a negative effect on those within earshot. Criticizing someone while there are customers nearby, as I have witnessed happening several times in retail establishments, reflects poorly on the entire organization. The old adage "Praise people in public, correct them in private" still holds true today.

If you want to improve productivity and well-being in your company, become a "goodness finder." Catch people doing things right and praise them for it. Organizations with large sales forces know the value of reward programs and use everything from books and gift cards to exotic trips as ways to motivate and reward their people for excellent performance.

It is equally important to motivate yourself in this way. When you do something really well or complete a task efficiently and on time, reward yourself. This could be anything from a simple cookie break for a small accomplishment to a weeklong vacation for accomplishing a major task.

Paying a simple compliment and saying "Good job" to someone goes a long way toward showing her that you recognize her accomplishments. And using personal rewards is a great way to help you overcome reluctance and embrace the task at hand. Focusing on the reward enables us to get through the work faster and with greater ease.

2. *Put Your Problems to Work for You*

I n his book *Illusions*, Richard Bach wrote, "There is no such thing as a problem without a gift for us in its hands. We seek problems because we need their gifts."

Whether or not we seek out problems is not nearly as important as how we handle them when they appear. A great technique I learned many years ago is to change the word *problem* to *challenge*. I realize this may seem like simply a matter of semantics, but hear me out.

Problems tend to be things we try to avoid, while challenges are things we step up to and fix. Making this seemingly insignificant change in vocabulary can have a big impact on how you deal with a situation.

If you view it, as Bach suggests, as having a gift for you or at least containing an opportunity within it, your challenge could be turned to your advantage. A challenge in the workplace, while representing an obstacle for some, can actually present you with an opportunity to showcase your talents. The next time a challenge presents itself, rather than trying to avoid it, welcome it. Ask yourself what you might do to turn it into an opportunity. Explore how you might best use it to your advantage.

A case in point is what happened when Domino's Pizza asked their customers how they liked their pizza. What they learned was that people didn't like it; they thought it was terrible and told the company so, by the thousands.

This must have hurt the folks at Domino's, but rather than bury their heads in the sand, as some companies do, they chose to embrace it. They made major changes to their product line and, from all indications, have transformed the company and won back customers with their improved pizza.

Making necessary changes can be difficult for many companies, as I'm sure it was for Domino's, but it pays off. When you and your team are faced with what appears to be a problem, try approaching it differently. Look at it as a challenge. Ask a better question. We'll explore the idea of powerful questions in chapter 15, but for now simply change the way you typically handle those less-than-desirable occurrences at work and, for that matter, in the rest of your life.

3. *Break Your Patterns*

It always amazes me how little people know about their company, coworkers, or the world around them. Many otherwise intelligent people become stuck in the rut of their daily lives, doing the same things each day, driving the same route to work, eating the same breakfast, and so on, rarely deviating from their patterns. In fact, we are all most likely to frequent the same five to ten restaurants, even though many communities have fifty or more.

We tend to eat the same five or six vegetables, even though there are more than ten times that to choose from. We drive the same roads to and from work, school, and home, hang out with the same friends, and engage in the same social events. We listen to the same music, watch the same TV shows, and on and on. It's no wonder people are bored.

If you want to have a happier, more interesting life at work and at home, start breaking your patterns. An added benefit is that you will be stimulating your creativity as a result. By changing your everyday patterns and habitual processes, you will be creating new neural connections in your brain.

Simply changing your route to and from work will expose you to new visual and auditory stimuli. As you drive, ride, or walk a new route, you will see things you have never noticed before. This is why so many creative people, Steven Spielberg among them, go for long drives in their cars to stimulate ideas.

Do you take the same actions in your work or business each day? Most of us follow certain routines, and while there is nothing wrong with this, doing so can stifle our creativity and prevent us from major breakthroughs. What could you do to shake up your routine? Could you change some of your daily actions? For example, would changing the way you handle email enable you to take a new action or complete a more urgent task? I found myself answering my email first thing in the morning, as though the sender was sitting there at 6:00 AM, waiting for my answer. This habit prevented me from doing something more important.

Scheduling a specific time to answer my email has freed up my early-morning time for writing, the most important component of my work. Morning is the time I write best, since my mind is still clear and calm after my morning meditation and quiet time. Delaying email until later in the morning has also provided me with the opportunity to get back to my morning exercise, another task that is critical to my well-being.

When I go out to do errands by car, if possible I follow a different route to my destination each time. Over time, I have found this time to be one of my best opportunities for brainstorming ideas. I can capture any new ideas I have in the car by dictating them into my iPhone.

The more you can shake up your routines, the more you will stimulate your creative mind. If you want to try an interesting experiment, when you're getting dressed in the morning put your pants on the opposite way from how you usually do it: if you usually place your right leg in first, this time put your left leg in first. Be sure to stand where you can sit quickly since this may well cause you to lose your balance — that is how strongly we are conditioned to our daily routines.

When you take a shower, wash your feet first instead of your face and notice how strange it feels. Take surface roads instead of the freeway next time you have to drive, and see how that feels.

The more you take advantage of opportunities to stimulate your mind, the more you will find new creative ideas popping into your head and the more likely you will be to produce breakthrough results.

4. *Become Curious*

If you want to be happier both at work and in your personal life, cultivate your curiosity. Not only will learning about the world and people around you make your job more interesting, but it will also increase your value to the company. As executive coach Jay Abraham put it, "Discovery is the fuel of competitive advantage."

The more you know about your company and its products and services, the more effectively and efficiently you will perform your work. This will lead to increased productivity and perhaps to a better position within the organization eventually. By cultivating your curiosity, you will be more engaged with your work and as a result feel like a more integral part of the organization.

Do you know the history of your company? Do you know who the CEO is or who the top management are? Depending on the size of your organization, these people may be across the corridor or across the globe. Even if they are far-flung, you can still learn about them. Many people I've met, especially in large organizations, do not even know the name of the chief executive.

Similarly, depending on the length of time your company has been in existence, there may be a rich or fascinating story behind it. It astonishes me how little most people know about the company they spend a third of their lives working for.

If you want to be happier and more successful in your career, learn what you can about your company. Make a point of learning something about the top management. If at all possible, meet the key executives. I realize that this may sound crazy, especially if you are in an entry-level position, but I assure you, you will benefit from the experience. You may be surprised how accessible and friendly the top people are. On top of that, I guarantee that your CEO will be impressed that you had the initiative to seek her out. This could be a huge help to your career.

By learning about and studying the history of your company, especially those who have been in the business for a few decades or more, you will learn how vital your role is and gain appreciation for what it took to build your company.

The result of this is that you will be happier and, according to most studies, your performance will increase. Since performance leads to advancement, expressing your natural curiosity will have a positive impact not only on your mood but on your career as well.

If you work for a large organization you may not have any idea about what the company's founder faced in the early days of trying to grow the business. For example, how many employees of the Ford Motor Company know that Henry Ford probably would not have built the Model T were it not for his wife's involvement. According to the story, as told by Napoleon Hill (author of *Think and Grow Rich*), Ford was having a hard time figuring out where to find the money to build the transmission, when his wife suggested he simply take it from his own savings and lend it to the company.

Employees of FedEx today have the pleasure of working for one of the world's most successful companies, but how many of them know that, in the early days, the company almost went out of business several times? There are stories of FedEx, during the early days, moving their planes around to keep them from being repossessed.

How many people working for KFC, formerly known as Kentucky Fried Chicken, know that its founder, Colonel Sanders, was bankrupt at age sixty-five when he began his now-famous chicken franchise?

Or how many Sears employees know that Richard Sears, the founder of Sears, Roebuck and Company, worked as a clerk on the railroad until one day when he had the opportunity to buy some watches, which he then sold at a fair price up and down the rail line?

I wonder how many Honda employees know that in the years following World War II, with gasoline in short supply and with most Japanese using bicycles as their main form of transportation, Soichiro Honda invented a small engine that attached to the bicycle, enabling it to go faster while still conserving fuel. That little engine was the beginning of the Honda Corporation.

What about your company? Whether it's large or small, I'm sure there's an interesting story about its beginnings. Knowing all you can about your company and its products and services will give you a sense of pride in your work, help make each day at work more enjoyable, and help you feel more connected to your work. Knowing about and, when possible, meeting your top executives will give you a better sense of who they are as people and gain you some insight into how they got where they are. They may even serve as role models for your career and contribute to your success.

5. *Know Your Purpose*

A number of years ago I was attending a talk given by Jack Canfield, cocreator of the Chicken Soup for the Soul series. It was a cold February night in New Jersey, and Jack was there as part of his national tour for his new book, *The Success Principles*.

As I was waiting for Jack to arrive I could not help but wonder why this famous author, who lives in Southern California, was in Edison, New Jersey, to speak to a small group of about forty people. It would have been so much easier for him to stay in the warmth of California instead of being here in the icy rain of a New Jersey winter. As Jack entered the room we shook hands and I told him how nice it was to see him again. Then I asked him why he was giving this talk.

Without hesitation he replied, "To change people's lives."

Jack clearly knew why he was doing the work he does. He knows what his purpose is and is dedicated to carrying out his mission — regardless of the weather.

What about you? Do you know why you do what you do?

Zig Ziglar, the late success legend, once said to an audience, "If you're going to a job today just because you went there yesterday, you may want to reconsider your life's plan."

Are you living your purpose? Perhaps the work you do is your purpose and passion, your gift to the world, so to speak. Or maybe you're still discovering what you truly want to do with your life.

Either way, understand that whatever you do and wherever you work right now is just what you need to be doing and just where you need to be at the moment. Though your job may only be a stepping-stone to where you are ultimately going, it's where you are at the moment, so you owe it to yourself and your employer to do your best work.

When Jack Canfield's publisher asked him to go on a book tour on the East Coast in the middle of winter, he didn't remind them he is a famous and wealthy author and say he would rather wait until spring. He went on the tour. Understanding his purpose in doing the work he does, he didn't hesitate. If you are truly committed to having a positive impact on people's lives, you do whatever it takes to accomplish that.

How does the work you do bring you satisfaction? How are you serving humanity? What could you do to feel even more satisfied from your work?

Regardless of how important or menial you feel your work is, it is an essential part of something bigger. When you understand this you will find it easier to derive pleasure and meaning from your work. You will feel better and, as a result, be happier. You may even be promoted!

6. *Step into the Career of Your Dreams*

Henry David Thoreau wrote this about pursuing dreams: "If one advances confidently in the direction of his dreams, and endeavors to live the life which he has imagined, he will meet with success unexpected in common hours."

Notice that he didn't say advance "sheepishly," "fearfully," or "timidly."

You were not born to live quietly, hoping to get to the end of your life without being noticed. Sadly, that's the way many people spend their lives. They simply plod along, working in a job that's not what they want, wishing they were someplace else, living, as Thoreau put it, "lives of quiet desperation."

Personally, I like this quotation from French writer Émile Zola: "If you ask me what I came into this life to do, I will tell you: I came to live out loud."

Are you living *your* life out loud?

Each one of us was born with different dreams and desires. Many teachings point to the idea that if you have a desire to be, do, or have something, you already possess the ability to make it a reality.

If you stop for a moment and think about your deepest desires, I think you'll agree that they are not only well within the realm of possibility but also within your present reach. You're probably a lot closer to achieving your dreams than you realize.

One problem, especially among creative types, is that it can be difficult to see how to turn what you love to do into a source of income, how to turn your passion into a career or business. This frustration, combined with all the technology and social media activity that seems essential to your success, leaves you feeling overwhelmed.

As Napoleon Hill wrote in *Think and Grow Rich,* success requires specialized knowledge; however, it does not have to come from you. You need to have the desire, willingness, and faith to take the first step. Once you've done that, the next steps will begin to appear. As Thoreau said, "If one advances confidently in the direction of his dreams…"

If you develop a strong commitment to your success and hold to your vision, taking whatever actions seem appropriate, you'll soon see the pieces coming together.

You'll meet the people necessary for you to progress, often in unusual ways. Resources will appear, seemingly out of nowhere. All sorts of occurrences will take place as the Universe conspires for your success, and, as our old friend Thoreau taught us, you will "meet with success unexpected in common hours."

So here it is in all its simplicity:

- Advance confidently, not fearfully.
- Endeavor to live the life you have imagined, the life you were born to live. Do your best.
- You will meet with success. Yes, you will.

7. *Make Your Dreams Come True*

One day a number of years ago, my wife, Georgia, observed that I wasn't having enough fun with money. Like a lot of people, I viewed money as something "serious" like bill paying and investing. She handed me a dollar bill with little smiley face stickers all over it as a reminder to be sure to use some of my money for fun.

It was a very good idea on Georgia's part, because every time I've opened my wallet since, I've seen all those smiley faces looking back at me. It's been a great reminder over many years to lighten up and enjoy my life.

Making small gestures such as putting smiley faces on dollar bills, taping pictures of the car you want to your mirror, and posting your sales goals in a prominent place will not in themselves bring you what you desire, but they will serve to keep your dreams and desires in the forefront of your mind and provide clear instructions to your subconscious about what you want. Creating visual representations of your desires is often referred to as making "treasure maps" or "dream boards or "vision boards."

Remember, your subconscious will act on whatever instructions you give it; however, it will not distinguish between what you say you want and what you say you don't want. It will not act on the reverse of an idea any more than you would be able not to think of the pink elephant if I were to say to you, "Don't think of a pink elephant." It won't work. For example, instead of saying, "I don't want all these bills," you might say, "I am debt-free and enjoying financial abundance."

Your subconscious takes everything you say, think, and feel literally, which is why you want to think, speak, and put your attention only on what you want to experience more of in your life.

It's why you want to talk about challenges rather than problems, and abundance rather than lack. As a matter of fact, if you perform applied kinesiology (muscle testing) on someone and then perform it again after she has repeated the phrase "I hate _____" a few times in a row, she will test weaker than she did the first time. However, if you perform this same test on someone who has repeated a sentence containing positive words, such as *love*, that person will test stronger the second time.

Words have power, and the words you speak have the power to add to or detract from your experience. If you want to enjoy a happier and more fulfilling life, be selective in what and who you listen to and even more selective in what you tell yourself. As the biblical proverb says, "The tongue has the power of life and death, and those who love it will eat its fruit" (18:21).

One of the most powerful things you can say (affirm) for yourself is, "My sales are steadily increasing as I add more value to my customers." Use this or something similar as your personal mantra, and watch your sales improve.

If you're experiencing financial challenges, try this affirmation from my colleague David Neagle: "I always have more than enough money."

I like this one a lot because it is clear and clean. It doesn't have any negative association or fixed number attached to it, while at the same time it affirms that you always have more than enough, which is just fine with me.

Use these and other positive affirmations, as well as dream boards and other visual reminders, to maintain a positive attitude and keep your life on track.

$8.$ *Become a Goal Setter*

I am astonished by the number of people I meet who do not regularly set goals. With all that has been written over the past hundred years about the value of having written goals, it's absurd that, according to all indications, only a very small percentage of the population make it a practice.

The fact that the people who make up this small percentage also tend to be the most successful is no big surprise. There's a clue in there: if you want more success, become a goal setter. As J. C. Penney put it, "Show me a stock clerk with goals and I'll show you a man who can make history. Show me a man without goals and I'll show you a stock clerk."

If there is one thing that has helped me realize my dreams in the past twenty-plus years, it's my regular practice of setting goals in various areas of my life.

During the first week of January every year, I jot down what I would like to accomplish in the year ahead. I begin by rereading my life's vision, a description of what my ideal life five years into the future looks like. This, of course, changes continually, since I always update it to reflect my current dreams and desires. In my ideal life vision I include my spiritual ideals, my health and fitness goals, my business and career goals, my personal relationship goals, my social and material goals, and, of course, my financial goals.

From there I make a list of everything I can think of that I would like in the coming year. This list serves as the basis for my top goals — the one or two important goals for each of the key areas of my life.

A lot has been written about the importance of goals and goal setting. Self-help guru Brian Tracy said, "People with clear, written goals accomplish far more in a shorter period of time than people who do not." This idea was originally alluded to by Aristotle and was later developed by Edward A. Locke and published as the article "Toward a Theory of Task Motivation and Incentives" in 1968.

Why is it important to set goals in the first place?

Setting goals for your life gives you a road map and a tool by which to gauge your progress. More important, it conveys your desire to your subconscious mind and to the Universe. You are declaring your intention to achieve the goal and, in many cases, by a particular date.

Personally, I treat goals as a guide to help me along the way. I do not obsess over whether or not I achieve a particular goal on the exact date I set but, more often than not, I manage to accomplish the goal on or before the date. If I don't, I do not abandon the goal; I simply move the date and make necessary adjustments.

Even if you fall short of a goal, you will still be far better off than if you had not set the goal in the first place. One year I set a goal to deliver fifty live seminars and talks. That would have meant I'd be speaking an average of once a week, an ambitious undertaking for most professional speakers. In reality, I delivered only thirty-five talks that year. Did I fail? I think not. Without that goal, how many times would I have spoken?

If you set a goal to earn $200,000 in a year's time and earn only $180,000, would you return the money, explaining that you missed your goal? Of course not. Even if all you do is write your goal on a sheet of paper and put it in a drawer, you'll still have a better chance of achieving it than if you never wrote it down in the first place.

In my opinion, if you keep your dreams and goals in your head, as so many people do, that's the only place they're likely to manifest. Writing them out has power. I believe that this has to do with the fact that writing goals takes them out of your mind and concretizes them in the physical realm. The process of writing out your goals makes them more real and provides you with a method of holding yourself accountable.

My Goal-Setting Process

In the process I use for goal setting, first, as mentioned above, I create as complete a picture as possible of my ideal life in each area five years from now. Then my goals are extracted from that. In this way I am assured that my goals are in alignment with my life's vision.

If you start with the goal first, you run the risk of ending up out of balance. Too many people set only money and achievement goals, ignoring areas such as health and family, and they wind up being unhappy. Enjoying the best life possible requires paying attention to several areas of your life simultaneously.

Once you have completed your vision you will have a picture of your ideal life in each key area. From there you can write one or two goals for each.

You will want to set some one-to-two-year goals based on your vision. In other words, for me to achieve my five-year career goals, what has to happen in the next one or two years? Later, we'll break this down further with a specific action plan (see chapter 10).

Looking at your life vision, focus on your vision for your career. In order for you to be living your compelling vision for your work in five years, what needs to happen in the next twelve to twenty-four months?

For example, if in your vision you are a first-line manager at work, what goal could you accomplish during the coming year? Perhaps you'll need more education. Maybe your company has a management succession program you can apply to attend.

If you are just starting out in or trying to break into a new career, you may be a long way from your ideal and worry that a better life is too far out of your reach. Keep in mind that, as has been written for centuries, a person can achieve anything he can conceive and believe.

As I mentioned earlier, if you have a strong desire for something, you already have within you the means to accomplish it. You would not have a true desire if the ability were not already there. God (however you may conceive of God) would not ignite a desire within you if realizing it were impossible. Your Creator does not tease.

Here are some specific guidelines for setting goals.

- Write your goals, either in your journal or on an electronic device. Personally, I write my goals in my journal, something I've been doing since 1987. Now that I use an iPad, I also store them electronically. That way they're always available to me to read and reflect on.

- Always write your goals in the first person and in the present tense: "I now have..." or "I am now..." You do not want to write "I will have"; since your subconscious mind does not judge, if you write your goal in the future tense, it will keep your goal out there, in the future.

- Try starting your goal with the phrase "I am so happy and grateful now that I am [fill in the goal]." I do this because it keeps the goal personal and in the present tense, and, more important, conveys my gratitude for what I am receiving.

If you want to attract more good into your life, cultivate a sense of gratitude for all that you already have, however small it may be. We will delve further into the power of gratitude in chapter 50.

9. *Don't Let Your Goals Scare You*

A re you playing too small?

It's fascinating to me that so many sales organization managers complain that their employees typically reach the quotas set by management, or perhaps even fall a bit short, but rarely exceed them. They get stuck in their comfort zone, setting and achieving smaller goals, ones that they know they can handle.

If you want to excel, set goals that cause you to stretch beyond your comfort zone and challenge you to step up.

You know what I mean: goals that both excite and scare you.

The thought of actually accomplishing them excites you, because it would be so fantastic. And the thought of even attempting to accomplish them scares you, because you still think you are not smart enough, skilled enough, or powerful enough, or some other illusion is stopping you. Remember that FEAR, or False Evidence Appearing Real, is just that — false evidence. You have no reason to fear attempting your most audacious goals, so why not just go for it?

It is likely that if the goal is big enough and important enough to you, you will find a way to accomplish it. If your desire is strong enough, you will be guided to the right resources, people, information, and actions to reach your objectives.

If you were to take off the restraints, what would you go for?

What goals would you strive to accomplish?

What great things would you attempt if you knew you would not fail?

What are you waiting for?

10. *Establish Milestones and Actions*

Now that you've written your compelling life vision and selected some goals you'd like to achieve in the next year, it's time to establish milestones and develop an action plan for accomplishing them.

Read back over your list of goals and, for each, write one or two milestones you can use to measure your progress. For example, if your vision includes rising to the top of your company and your goal is to become a manager within the next one to two years, your ninety-day milestone may be to have completed your next-level certification. This becomes a kind of mini-goal you will reach on your way to your main objective.

If in your vision you're the top salesperson in your company and one of your goals is to be number one in your district by the end of next year, your ninety-day milestone measurement might be to become number one in your region.

Once you have listed your ninety-day milestones for your goals, it's time to add actions you can take in the next thirty days to move you toward your desires. For, as the Bible has it, "Faith without works is dead" (James 2:17).

Write a few steps you can take in the next month to move you closer to reaching your goals. For now, simply list whatever you can think of that you can do. From this list you will determine the weekly and daily actions and activities that are necessary to move you in the direction of your ideal life vision.

Include at least one thing you can do immediately to get you going. It is vital, when setting goals, to take an immediate action. This gives your subconscious mind a clear message that you are serious about this endeavor. Too many people make New Year's resolutions or set weak goals and then do nothing after that. Obviously, they rarely accomplish what they set out to do. More often than not, these well-intentioned resolutions fall by the wayside by the time the champagne goes flat.

By attaching one or two small actions to your goals, you are establishing your intention to achieve them. As you will read in chapter 55, intention is a very powerful tool.

Don't be concerned if you're not sure exactly what you'll need to do to reach your goals. Most likely you won't know — if you did, you already would have achieved them. At this stage you just need to know what you want and why, and to start moving in the direction of your dreams. Simply keep your eye on your desire, seeing it as already fulfilled, and trust in God, Creator, Spirit, or whatever name you give to your Higher Power.

Reaching your goal will probably require some specialized knowledge, but it does not all need to come from *you*. Whatever you need to accomplish your goal is already here. You will attract the people with the skills and experience you require to achieve your outcome as you move toward your desire.

People who use some kind of formal goal setting know that once we start moving toward what we want, unexpected events occur and people show up in our lives and facilitate the successful achievement of our goals.

Before you complete the process of listing your actions, be sure to read the following chapter, about the difference between action and "inspired action." That chapter alone can help you increase your results by leaps and bounds.

11. *Take Only Inspired Action*

In my work, whether writing, speaking, or coaching, I distinguish between two distinctly different types of action. The first is what I refer to as "gerbil action."

This is the name I ascribe to what too many people do. Most of us have been taught to take a lot of action if we want to achieve a particular result. We have financial services representatives who make a hundred phone calls an hour selling their services. Outside sales representatives in many industries, especially advertising sales, plod along each day, going from business to business, cold calling in the hope of making a sale, much like Willy Loman, the depressing character in the Arthur Miller play *Death of a Salesman*.

This type of activity makes you feel busy but often produces little return on your effort. Repeated long enough, it results in lowered morale, depression, and, ultimately, job burnout. Companies that encourage "action, action, action" behavior typically suffer high turnover and mediocre outcomes.

I call this behavior gerbil action because it reminds me of a little gerbil spinning on his wheel and going nowhere. While I have nothing against gerbils, there is a better way. This brings us to the second type of action.

A number of years ago I was part of a small group of professional coaches taking an advanced training taught by two of the top coaches in the field. We were studying the laws of the Universe and how they work in our lives. This was a coaching program for businesses, combining the principles of the law of attraction with traditional business-building strategies. Clients who used this method enjoyed quantum leaps in revenue.

We were taught a strategy referred to as "inspired action." This action taps into the higher forces that are available to assist us on our journeys — it's a kind of prayer, if you will. What you are doing is asking for help from your Higher Power. How you view that Power is your choice, based on your beliefs.

What makes inspired action different is the way you approach it. My process is this:

Choose a particular area of your job or a task you would like to complete. Write a simple, short vision statement, acting as if the task has already been completed in an easy and effortless manner. I use a large index card or tablet for this.

Then, whenever you are going to work on this particular task, read your vision statement, seeing and feeling the successful completion. In reality the task is already perfect and complete on the level of creation. Your job is to bring its completion into physical existence.

Once you have read your vision and can imagine it having already been completed, then and only then ask your Higher Power what next action will bring you closer to the successful completion of the task.

Then sit quietly and wait for an inspiration. Listen to and trust your intuition, that small voice that whispers to you when you're quiet. I promise you that the ideas that come to you will be different from what you would receive if you simply acted without first aligning your energy with your desires.

You may be inspired to call someone you haven't spoken with for a while. You may feel inclined to write a letter or send an email. Whatever inspiration you receive, act on it as soon as possible. As my colleague Joe Vitale has said many times, "The Universe loves speed."

12. *Align with Your Values*

O ur values are one of the most important components of personal development, yet we often overlook them. By *values* I
mean those principles and qualities that you hold dear. We all have
a set of values — such as love, success, compassion, freedom, contribution, adventure, and security — that are important to us and
determine our happiness. That is, our happiness or satisfaction in
any situation depends on our most important values being met. And
our behavior in any situation will be directly related to our particular
set of values. Identifying and understanding your values will go a
long way toward helping you create a life of joy and happiness.

Additionally, we attach importance to these values in a particular order and, as you'll see below, have established "rules" that
govern what has to happen for us to experience a particular value
as being met. Do not be concerned if this sounds complicated. It is
really pretty simple, as you will see as we go on.

Uncovering Others' Values — and Your Own

Understanding other people's values will improve communication
and, in the workplace, will enable you to understand what drives
your colleagues and how best to work with them. In business and
sales, identifying a person's values will raise you from being an

ordinary salesperson to one who truly serves the customer. You will know how to present your product or service to address your customer's most important concerns.

As a manager, if you ask an employee, "What's most important to you in your work?" her first answer will, most likely, reveal her number one career value. If you continue to ask the question (e.g., "What else is important to you at work?"), you will uncover the other values that are important to her. For example, if her first answer to the question is "security," you know that this is probably her number one value. If you continue asking, you will uncover more of her values, such as contribution, recognition, success, money, challenges, and so on.

Once you have your list, to really get to know your employee, you will begin asking which value is more important. For example, you might ask, "Is contribution more or less important than recognition?" If she were to answer, "Contribution is more important," you might then ask, "Is success more or less important than contribution?" If it were less, you would ask, "Is success more or less important than recognition?" By doing this you come to understand the order in which this employee values these different things. You know already that security is her number one value since it was the first thing that came to her. Of course, you can easily check that by asking her to compare it to her other values.

Once you have elicited this list of values and their order of importance, you've gained quite a bit of insight into what drives your employee's behavior. As her manager, you now know how to better motivate her and what types of assignments will best suit her. If her number one value is adventure and there is an opportunity for someone to go to a distant land and open a new office, she'll be your ideal choice. On the other hand, if her number one value is family, she's not going to be suited for this assignment, unless her family can travel too.

Whether or not you manage other people, it is a good idea to invest time in uncovering your own values, since they will determine your level of happiness. One of the reasons that so many people are unhappy is that their lives are out of alignment with their core values.

For example, someone whose number one value is freedom but has a job that requires him to work in an office with a structured schedule will most likely be unhappy. Someone whose top value is freedom may be happier in a position that allows him to be out of the office and to structure his day according to his needs. Your typical business-development people, working outside the office and running their own schedule, are generally those who value freedom highly.

One of my high-priority values is contribution. Because of this, I know I would not be happy or feel satisfied in any position that did not allow me to make a contribution. One of the reasons I love to write is that it allows me to give to humanity. I feel that what I write will help other people become happier and more successful, and that makes me happy.

Be aware that your values will change over time. A high-priority value for a young unmarried person on a career fast track may shift as that person gets married and has a family. The values that inspired the entrepreneur will shift as he or she becomes more successful. Often people who have become highly successful devote their time to serving their community. While achievement or success may have originally been their number one value, as they reached a certain level of success, their values changed. It is a worthwhile exercise to reassess your values every few years to see how they have evolved.

Values in Business

As noted above, understanding people's values can be quite helpful when you are managing them. It is also an asset in sales. If I am presenting my product or service to you, and have taken the time to uncover your top values, I can match the benefits of my product to your values. This will provide you with a higher level of service and will increase the likelihood of my making a sale, since I am addressing what's most important to you.

People buy things for their own reasons. Knowing what motivates the buyer, I can demonstrate how my product or service aligns with her values. The more she sees the value in it for herself, the more likely she is to buy.

Let's look at an example. Suppose I am selling luxury automobiles. As a result of asking you, "What's most important to you in an automobile?" I learn that your number one value is safety for your family. Knowing this, I will concentrate my presentation on the safety features of the car and point out each of the safety and security benefits of owning it.

On the other hand, if I learn that your top value in a car is style or luxury, I will change my presentation to emphasize the car's comforts and its elegant appearance. I may point to the leather interior and the enhancements that separate it from other, less stylish automobiles.

The Lost Sale

I once visited a luxury car dealer on a quiet Saturday morning. It was quite early and there was no one in the showroom but a lone salesperson and me. He politely asked if he could help me. I pointed to a car on the showroom floor and asked what colors it came in. The salesman ignored my question. He had just returned from a training seminar where he had learned all the safety features of the car, and he proceeded to tell me, in great detail, how safe this automobile was.

He went on and on, totally disregarding what was important to me, because he, not I, was interested in the safety of the vehicle. I thanked him and left. It's not that I don't care about safety; I do. It's just that I assume an expensive car is well built and safe. Besides, I do not buy a car with the thought of crashing it. All I wanted to know was what colors were available. Had he simply answered my question and addressed my number one value instead of his own, he may have made the sale.

Understanding another person's values increases your ability to effectively communicate with him. Understanding your own values enables you to make decisions that will leave you feeling happier and more fulfilled. It is quite simple: if you make a decision that is out of alignment with your top values, you will be unhappy, no matter what else you do. If you align your life and work with your unique order of values, you will be happier and more productive, and you will enjoy a more satisfying and fulfilling life.

Activity Step: Uncovering Your Values

In your journal answer the following questions:

- What five values are most important to me in my life?
- What five values are most important to me in my work?

Next, prioritize your personal value list by asking, "Is this more important than that?" and so on until you have ranked the values in order of importance.

13. *Discover Your Rules*

No discussion about values would be complete without talking a little bit about the rules we each assign to experiencing a value — what has to happen for us to feel that a particular value is being met. Say the value in question is receiving recognition. For one person to feel his contribution is receiving recognition may require him to be praised in front of the team, while another individual may be fine with being texted, "Good job." Understanding other people's rules, especially those closest to you, can go a long way toward ensuring better communications and more harmonious relationships.

Pulling Your Own Strings

You can increase the likelihood of bringing about your desired states simply by making sure your rules for them are easy to follow. For example, if you want to be happy, make it easy for yourself. If your rule for experiencing happiness was something like "Every day above ground is a happy day," you would feel happy most of the time. Some people have so many rules for what makes them happy that happiness becomes almost impossible to achieve, so they spend their lives being miserable.

On the other side of the coin, you'll want to make it difficult or impossible to experience the feeling of failure. My personal rule for failure is that in order to experience it, I would have to completely give up. Since I'm not about to do that, it is virtually impossible for me to fail. Sure, I may experience setbacks. Not everything I do works out according to plan. However, I believe it all happens for a reason and there is something for me to learn from every experience, regardless of the outcome. After all, many times I have been in a situation that could have been considered a total failure, but it turned out to be the best thing that could have happened to me.

Years ago, when I woke up in a hospital bed, spiritually, mentally, physically, and financially bankrupt as a result of the excessive lifestyle habits I had developed, I thought my life was over. In reality, it was the best thing that has ever happened to me, pulling me up from a life that had been miserable and allowing me to do the work I do now. Had I not hit that bottom, I would have never asked for the help I needed with my problem and had the spiritual rebirth I've experienced, nor would I have been able to touch the lives of so many people with my work. A big part of why people like my books and programs is that they know I have been through the pain and that I walk my talk. I use all the principles I write about, and my life keeps getting better and better.

Activity Step: Discovering Your Rules

In your journal, next to the list of values you wrote earlier, write one or two things that have to happen for you to feel that each value has been met.

14. *Learn to Manage Your Time*

I t seems as though everyone I talk to these days is stressed-out trying to accomplish all the things their busy lifestyles demand. Between working long hours, attending endless meetings, managing multiple projects (each with its own stressors), dealing with the never-ending onslaught of email, maintaining our business network and connections on social media, and, oh, yeah, trying to have some semblance of a personal life, we are all stretched to the limit.

How is it, then, that some people seem to have plenty of time to accomplish everything, with time left over, while the rest of us rush around all day and never seem to have enough time?

One of the areas a lot of people, including myself at one time, seem to have trouble with is finding time to exercise regularly. With all the demands being made on us daily, exercise is often the first thing to go, when in fact it is one of the most important things we can do for ourselves. When I was having difficulty making time to take care of my physical health I did what I typically do in these situations: I sought the advice of someone who was achieving excellence in this area. In my case, I went to my friend Jim Sutton. Jim is a very successful and busy attorney yet manages to find the time to work out almost every day. When I asked him how, with all his other responsibilities, he could find the time to work out so often, his answer was quite simple. He said, "I make it one of the three most important things I must do each day." There's his secret — priorities!

Notice he didn't say it's one of the items on his ten-item to-do list. It was one of his top three.

Many busy people tend to make long lists of what they need to accomplish in a given day. They then become totally stressed-out trying to accomplish more than is reasonably possible in the time allotted.

If you study highly productive people you'll find that most make a list of the five most important things that they need to do that day, and do nothing else until those five are completed, instead of writing long lists and then becoming frustrated when they can't get it all done.

Each week I meet with my friend and coach Ski Swiatkowski, and we coach each other on what needs to happen for us to reach our goals in our respective businesses. An important component of this process is making a commitment to doing certain things in the upcoming week. A huge benefit of having a coach is accountability to another person for doing what needs to be done. In our sessions we each commit to at least three things that will have the greatest impact on our success.

If you want to accomplish more, feel better, and be less stressed, make a habit of writing down the three to five most important things you need to do each day to achieve your goals — and do nothing else until they are completed.

This seemingly simple act can greatly boost your success and enable you to accomplish the tasks that are truly important to your future. Each day, make a list — in your journal, your tablet, or your computer — of no more than five tasks that are the most important for you to do that day. Do them before anything else, and watch your productivity soar.

Another great productivity tip, taken from Brian Tracy's book *Eat That Frog*, is to do the one thing that you'd rather not deal with before you do anything else. The personal power you'll feel when you do this will motivate you to take on the remainder of your tasks for the day.

15. *Ask a Bigger Question*

I believe it was Mark Victor Hansen, cocreator of the wildly successful Chicken Soup for the Soul book series, who said, "If you want a bigger result, ask a bigger question."

If you listen to people's conversations, particularly around the water cooler, you'll hear an endless diatribe of disempowering questions such as, "Why do I get all the lousy assignments?" and "Why don't I ever get a break?"

Asking focused and well-formed questions is one of the most powerful techniques we can employ in any situation, especially in the workplace. Try using a series of empowering questions first thing in the morning as a way to start off your day feeling good about yourself and the day ahead.

Simple questions such as, "What am I looking forward to today?" "What am I happy about today?" and "What am I grateful for today?" will enable you to begin your day on a more positive note.

Unfortunately, too many people ask questions such as, "Why do I have to go to work today?" "Why do I have to get out of bed so early?" and other disempowering ones that do little more than undermine what good feelings they may have had and put them in a less-than-great mental state as they begin their day. Right from the start they are defending their lack of success with a "why me?" attitude.

After all, they think, rich and successful people don't have to get up early and get to work. Of course, nothing could be further from the truth; highly successful people are typically the first ones in the office in the morning because they are excited about their work and their lives.

If you want to escape this trap and be happier and more productive at work and in your life overall, begin to formulate better questions. We human beings are conditioned to ask and answer questions. Whether or not you agree with that statement, you had to ask yourself a question about how you felt about it in order to form your opinion. If you ask someone a question, chances are she will respond. Even Yogi Berra, when asked, "What time is it?" responded, "You mean now?"

You can learn to harness this powerful questioning technique to foster good feelings and increase your success on a particular project.

At work make a habit of formulating powerful, intuitive questions such as, "How could I do this better and more effectively?" and "What's great about this situation?" By making a habit of using powerful, positive, engaging questions daily, you will take a huge step in managing communication with yourself and in making yourself feel better in any given situation.

If, for example, you work in sales and your monthly goal is to add three new customers, you might formulate a question such as, "What could I do this month that would result in adding twelve new customers?" This question would force your mind to come up with a very different answer than if you were to ask how to acquire three. Remember, "If you want a bigger result, ask a bigger question."

I believe that one of the problems individuals and companies have is the habit of asking small, uninspiring questions that, in turn, produce small results. When I published my first book one of my core questions was, "What can I do to sell a million books?" This was beyond bold, considering that the average book if its type sells maybe a couple of thousand copies and that I knew nothing about book selling at the time.

Looking back, asking that question was one of the smartest things I ever did, because it forced me to look at book marketing differently and, in turn, to take actions that were markedly different from the norm.

The result? In my first year in the publishing industry, we sold more than one hundred thousand copies of *Handbook to a Happier Life*. This made me an instant celebrity among small publishers and enabled me to build a career as an author.

In your company, instead of asking what you could do in order to be promoted to your boss's level, you might ask, "What steps would I need to take in order to become qualified to rise three levels above my current level?" A question of this type would, by necessity, cause your mind to churn out answers that are radically different from those that would follow a "smaller" question.

Make a practice of tapping into the enormous capability of your mind by asking focused questions. And "If you want a bigger result, ask a bigger question."

Activity Step: Asking the Right Questions

- Write four or five empowering questions you can ask to start off your day on the right foot.
- What new question could you apply to your greatest work challenge right now?

16. *Arrive at Work Early*

If you want to be happier and more productive at work and have less stress in your life, stop rushing. Disengage from the very idea of *rush hour*, a term that at its very core is counterproductive. You get to choose how you feel when you begin your workday. You can follow the herd and rush each morning, or you can begin your day in an easier and more relaxed manner.

A number of years ago I took a freelance assignment teaching computer software at a technology school about thirty miles from my home. After the first few days of driving in heavy commuter traffic during the morning rush hour, I became determined to find a better way.

One morning I decided to leave my home twenty minutes earlier just to see what effect that might have on my trip. It turned out to be the ideal solution. Because I left for work a bit earlier, I was just ahead of the big traffic buildup. In my case this meant thousands of commuters heading toward Philadelphia, the fifth largest city in America.

Depending on where you live, your plan would need to be adjusted for your local conditions. My leaving home just twenty minutes ahead of what would have been the normal time to leave enabled me to enjoy a leisurely drive in light to moderate traffic.

As it turned out, my travel time was reduced by another twenty minutes, giving me time to relax and enjoy a morning coffee. The added benefit of my arriving early, aside from my being more relaxed and not feeling stressed, was that because I had the extra forty minutes, I could work on my own writing. As a result I completed my second book.

How much better would you feel if you could ease into your day, arriving at your workplace with plenty of time to spare? How would it feel to be relaxed on your journey, knowing you had ample time instead of being one of the harried, stressed-out commuters that you see in any city in the world, early on a workday.

Why not give yourself the gift of an enjoyable morning commute? All it takes is a little planning and the willingness to leave a bit earlier. You will begin your day relaxed and be in a physical and mental state to be more productive. (You may even decide to write a book.)

And if you make use of your travel time by listening to audio programs and podcasts, you can turn your car into a "university on wheels." Over time this practice will enable you to become knowledgeable about almost any subject you wish to learn.

17. *Master Your Energy*

To be truly happy, productive, and successful, you need physical, mental, and emotional energy. Unfortunately, for many people, just mustering enough energy to get through the day can be a major task. If you take the time to examine the lifestyle and habits of today's typical individual, it's not hard to see why so many people have difficulty.

Often people are jolted awake, after too little sleep, by an alarm clock. Their waking thoughts are usually about how they wish they didn't have to wake up so early.

Rushing into their day, many opt for a fast-food breakfast, typically consisting of coffee or some other caffeinated drink and a bagel, muffin, doughnut, or some heavy carbohydrate, often eaten and drunk while en route to work. Now their insulin level is artificially spiked, causing a rise in blood sugar. They are in a mental fog from their high-carb intake (not to mention the fact that over time this kind of diet can lead to obesity and diabetes). On their way to work they are either on their cell phone or beginning to worry about what they need to do that day. Since they were rushed from the start, they probably left for work late, so they are also worried about their tardiness.

Their stress level is already dangerously high — and they haven't even arrived at work yet.

They manage to survive till their first break, at which time another shot of caffeine with a side of carbs gives them a much-needed spike so they can make it until lunchtime. During this break they may also engage in several conversations with negative coworkers about what's wrong with the company, their job, and the world in general.

As far-fetched as this scenario may sound, it's a fairly accurate description of an average employee's morning. With a few variations, this cycle continues until, exhausted at the end of the day, he flops into bed to try to get a decent night's sleep, but not before watching the late-night news on TV just to make sure that he's gotten his dose of negativity for the day.

Is it any wonder that so many people are burned-out, angry, depressed, and aging faster than they ever thought possible?

Here are some suggestions to help you break that pattern, feel better, and have more energy throughout your day.

- For starters, make sure you get enough sleep. Most people require at least seven to eight hours of uninterrupted sleep.
- To help you get adequate sleep, avoid caffeine in the evening. The effects of caffeine remain in your system for about six to seven hours after you consume it.
- Make a point of having a high-protein breakfast. This will give your body what it needs to get going.
- As suggested in chapter 15, before you get out of bed, ask yourself one or two empowering questions such as, "What am I grateful for today?" or "What am I looking forward to today?" This will start your mind moving in a more positive direction, and because like attracts like, these questions will begin inspiring similar thoughts.
- Leave yourself plenty of time for your commute. Arriving early gives you time to settle in before you start your workday.
- Do your best to avoid the negative conversations that exist in

just about every company. We'll discuss this in detail later in the book (see chapter 56).

- If you must watch the evening news, or read a news website or newspaper, do it earlier in the evening. The last thing you want to do is take all that horror and negativity into your dream state.

Just making these relatively simple changes to your lifestyle will go a long way toward raising your energy level and helping you feel better both at work and at home.

18. *Commit to Lifelong Learning*

This is perhaps one of the most important commitments you can make if you want to be on a happier, more productive, and more fulfilling career path.

The statistics about how many books people read after completing their formal education are appalling. Upon graduation, colleges and universities hold commencement ceremonies. The word *commencement* itself holds the clue that your life is beginning and that your education, rather than coming to an end, should be commencing as well.

If you study successful people in any walk of life, you will find that they are continual learners and avid readers. Every high-achieving individual I've ever met reads personal-development and business books regularly. They continually listen to audio seminars and podcasts, and they attend live seminars, where they not only gain new knowledge but also meet and network with other successful people.

Many of the largest, most successful companies in the world encourage people to participate in a book-of-the-month club. They know that the more their employees work on their personal development, the better the company will perform. If you want to lead a fulfilling and successful life, make a daily habit of reading good books.

The information you learned in school was just the beginning. It will not carry you into the future. Rather, the learning you acquire regularly is what will determine how far and how high you reach in your work life. It's not something that you were taught in school a decade ago. This is one of the reasons that many people with little formal education have reached high levels of success in business and in life.

Commit now to reading for at least ten to fifteen minutes a day. Read a book or more each month, and listen to audios and podcasts in your area of interest. Attend seminars, teleseminars, and webinars to continually sharpen your skills and maintain your positive attitude, because, as the title of my friend Jeff Keller's book suggests, *Attitude Is Everything*.

My friend the late Charlie "Tremendous" Jones, a personal-development legend, taught us, "You will be the same person in five years as you are today except for the people you meet and the books you read."

19. *Become a Value Finder*

It's unfortunate that, in many organizations, the only time people hear from their superiors is when they've made a mistake. Too many managers and supervisors spend their days searching for someone who's done something wrong and, when they find him or her, pounce on that person like a hungry cat after a mouse.

While this may solve an immediate problem, in the long run it makes for a very unpleasant work environment.

If you want to be happier and more productive and to rise in your company faster, become a "value finder." Value finders are those people who are always on the lookout for an opportunity to compliment their coworkers and employees. They actively seek people who are doing things right and make a practice of praising them, usually in earshot of others in the department.

Companies that encourage value finding throughout the organization typically find not only that morale improves significantly but also that productivity improves as well. Happy people perform better than unhappy people. It's that simple.

Let's face it: no one likes to be berated in front of others for making a mistake. It's embarrassing, and, to a great extent, will lower the morale of the entire organization.

Of course, people need to be corrected from time to time; however, a better way to do this is by acting in a coaching capacity rather than by just pointing a finger and, figuratively, beating up on the individual. And it should always be done in private. As stated earlier, never criticize or critique an employee in front of other people in the group.

Fred has a habit of being late most days. A lot of managers would simply scold him, hopefully in private, and tell him to make sure he was on time in the future, or they might even threaten him with dismissal. Neither of these, by the way, would do much for improving his motivation or morale.

A manager acting in a coaching capacity would first ask Fred what he thought the cause of his perpetual tardiness was. This is a more constructive approach to the problem, since it addresses the underlying cause of the behavior rather than the behavior itself. The manager may learn, for example, that Fred has to drop his children off at school and if he could come in even a half hour later, it would ease the situation. In many instances this would be an easy enough change to make.

Whatever the problem, the manager who can act in a coaching capacity is more likely to remedy the problem, since she is addressing the situation causally.

There was a time in history, not that long ago, when people believed that berating their employees and, unfortunately, their children, was the way to improve performance. We now know better. Putting a person down for making a mistake is, as mentioned earlier, like hitting your computer with a stick to make it work better. You wouldn't even consider hitting your MacBook with a stick, yet we do the equivalent to our employees, coworkers, spouses, and children all the time.

The boss or manager who becomes known as someone who catches people doing things right and comments about it cultivates a culture of support and recognition in the department and quickly rises in the organization.

Companies are once again appreciating the value of their employees and understanding that the time and resources invested in their development and well-being contributes directly to the bottom line. In the twenty-first century, your most valuable asset is what comes in the door every morning and goes home at the end of the day: namely, your employees and colleagues.

If you take care of them, the company will reap the benefits of an empowered and inspired workforce.

20. *Don't Be Afraid to Speak Your Mind*

Many years ago I attended a meeting in the office of one of my clients. At the time I owned a marketing and advertising agency and was invited to the meeting to share my ideas on how the company might position its new technology product. This was the early 1990s, an exciting time, since technology was about to explode.

In attendance were the company president, the executive team, myself, and another outside consultant who had initially brought me into the company to help with new product launches.

The president was proposing his ideas about what to call the company's latest breakthrough product and how best to proceed. It was obvious to my friend Bill and I that he had no idea how to successfully launch the product and that if his suggestions were implemented, the launch would never succeed. The president went on and on about how we should do this and that and how the project should be carried out.

Looking around the room I saw the various key executives nodding in agreement with his ideas. The only ones not nodding were Bill and I. We knew the ideas would not work.

Looking back, I realize the others knew it too, but none of them spoke up. Either they were worried that disagreeing with the boss might cost them their jobs, or they simply wanted to make the boss like them by agreeing with his ideas, however absurd.

Fortunately for the organization, Bill voiced his objections. He said that as a consultant he was being paid for his opinion and that if he didn't speak up he'd be shortchanging the company. He essentially told the president, in polite terms, that the ideas he was suggesting would not work. He then went on to explain why.

I'll never forget the look on the faces of the managers in attendance. They could not believe that someone would have the audacity to contradict the company's founder and chief executive. I think they were waiting for Bill to be fired and thrown out of the meeting.

Instead, the president laughed and thanked my friend for his courage in speaking out and, after listening to Bill's reasons for opposing the idea, agreed that his own ideas would, in fact, most likely not work.

Successful businesspeople know that they are not infallible and will respect you for voicing an opposing opinion. Of course, be sure to do so respectfully. No one in a top position really wants a bunch of yes men or women in the organization. If they do, you can be pretty certain that the company will not succeed. I'm sure there are examples that prove the opposite but, for the most part, true leaders expect to be wrong some of the time and rely on their employees to point out when they are.

If you find yourself in a situation where disagreeing with your boss is in the best interest of the organization, do it. Of course, it is best done in private, when possible. No one, even a tough business leader, likes to be corrected publicly. The exception to this practice is during high-level management meetings like the one described above. In these situations, disagreement and intense debate are expected.

Companies need leaders, people who are willing to speak their minds, even if it means contradicting their bosses, so long as it is the best interest of the organization.

If you want to be happier and more successful in your work, don't be afraid to speak your mind. Of course, don't forget that you are not infallible, either.

21. *Dress for Success*

When I was in the early stages of putting my life back together after having hit my personal bottom, one of the programs that had a huge impact on me, and was the catalyst for what has become my life's work, was an audio by Denis Waitley titled *The Psychology of Winning*.

On one of the cassettes, Dr. Waitley talked about positive self-image and, in one segment, stated that one key to improving your self-image was to "dress and look your best at all times." While this may seem obvious, this practice can have a profound effect on how you feel about yourself and the way you project yourself to the outside world.

While it is said that "the clothes do not make the woman" (or man) and "you don't judge a book by its cover," in practice the opposite is usually true. We typically judge people by their appearance. And, as anyone in the book industry will tell you, book covers are one of the most important considerations when publishing a book.

It may seem pretty superficial to judge someone by her appearance; however, it's what we do, consciously or unconsciously. First impressions are important, and the first thing someone will notice about you is how you look. It's human nature. It has been said that we form an opinion about a person in the first thirty seconds after meeting him. This is why it is so important, especially at work, to look and dress your best at all times.

Wear stylish clothes that fit properly, complement your natural appearance, and, of course, are appropriate for your job. Pay attention to your personal appearance, making sure your hair is neat and clean. Women need to ensure that their makeup, if they wear any, is appropriate for the work environment.

Years ago we hired a local home-improvement contractor to do some work in our home. The contractor, Tom, arrived in a clean, detailed van and was dressed in a clean, smartly pressed uniform with his company logo embroidered on the shirt pocket. Just his appearance made us feel comfortable and communicated the image of a confident, successful professional. Over the years, Tom has helped us with several projects and is someone I would refer to others without hesitation.

If you work in an office or are in sales, invest in a good-quality wardrobe. If you need to do this on a budget, shop the outlet stores or even high-end consignment shops. In my book *Stop Living Paycheck to Paycheck*, I tell the story of the insurance salesman who would buy designer suits in a consignment store, wear them a couple of times, and then resell them on eBay. Doing this enabled him to dress quite expensively without spending a fortune and had the added effect of impressing his clients. It is a fact that people like to do business with successful people.

Here's a tip from my wife, Georgia. If you want to rise in an organization, look at how your boss's boss dresses, and model that.

And remember what movie mogul Darryl Zanuck said: "Never make a deal with a man in a cheap suit."

22. Don't Wait to Be Told What to Do

One thing that has helped me in my work life more than anything else is my natural tendency to do whatever needs to be done without waiting to be told.

I'm not exactly sure when this trait was instilled in me, but for as long as I can remember, this is how I've been. From my teenage years, while working at part-time jobs and attending school, to this day, my natural tendency is to take charge. This trait has served me well throughout my working life.

Too many people in the workplace wait around for someone to tell them what to do next. Leaders, on the other hand, take initiative and, recognizing what needs to be done, take charge and ensure that the work is completed. Leaders do not wait to be told what to do. They act.

I'm suggesting not that you exceed your authority and do what you choose but that, within the scope of your responsibility, you do more than what is expected of you.

Years ago there was a television sitcom called *Chico and the Man*, starring the late Freddie Prinze. In the show one of the most memorable lines was "It's not my job, man!" The line, Puerto Rican accent and all, became part of the vernacular at the time and for years afterward. In offices all over, people would repeat it, usually in a whisper, whenever their boss told them to do something.

Unfortunately, it spawned an attitude that prevails to this day. The "It's not my job" attitude is what keeps people from advancing in their careers. If you want to rise in your organization, take ownership of your job and make as many things as possible part of your area of responsibility. Of course, I'm not suggesting you become obsessed with work. We all require balance in our lives in order to be at our best.

We desperately need leaders, people who behave as if everything is part of their job description and who not only perform their required duties but also look for additional ways to be of more value to their employer. If you lead in this way your efforts will be recognized and rewarded by your superiors. People notice those who consistently exceed what is expected of them. They also notice the slackers.

If you want to be happier, make your work more enjoyable, and rise within your organization, become someone who looks for ways to improve the organization, whether or not it is within the scope of your job description. An added benefit to becoming this type of worker is that you will find your day-to-day work more challenging and enjoyable.

Make a practice of looking around your department and see where you can add value. Become self-motivated and look for ways to improve, even if it's something as simple as making a pot of coffee instead of waiting for someone else to do it.

I've noticed over the years that many high-level executives will do the most menial tasks simply because the tasks need to be done. Leaders do not wait for someone else to do things. They take action. That's why they're leaders.

A number of years ago Georgia and I were vacationing in San Francisco, one of our favorite places to visit. We had just finished a wonderful dinner at Ernie's Restaurant, which was at the time one of the top restaurants in the city. (As a matter of fact, it's where I proposed to Georgia.) As we were leaving I realized there were no taxis around since the restaurant was not on a main road. Looking around, I noticed a well-dressed man standing near the entrance, reading over the reservation book, so I approached him and asked if he could help us hail a cab. He replied that he'd be happy to help. He went outside and, with a whistle, managed to get us a taxi to take us back to our hotel. When I got in the cab, Georgia was laughing. As it turned out, the man I had asked to hail us a taxi was the owner of one of the finest restaurants in a city famous for great restaurants. She couldn't believe I had asked him to hail us a cab. My reasoning was simple — he wasn't doing anything else and we needed a ride. Even though he was the owner, he didn't hesitate to help a customer, despite the fact that it was clearly not his "job."

23. *Focus on What Is Working*

I n his wonderful book *Breaking the Rules*, Kurt Wright writes about employing intuitive questioning as a means to solving problems within an organization.

One of the key questions, which I consider quite powerful and which I use regularly, is "What's working?" In any situation, either at work or in your personal life, you can use this value-finding question to tap into your creativity and solve problems, regardless of their scope.

We tend to do the opposite. We typically look at what's wrong in a situation and attempt to solve it from that perspective. The problem with that, as they say in New England, is that "you can't get there from here." You cannot be on the same wavelength of the problem and expect to devise effective solutions. It's as Albert Einstein said: "You cannot solve a problem from the same consciousness that created it."

By shifting your focus from what's wrong to what's working, you will be able to tap into your intuitive, creative right brain and to find new ways of accomplishing your objective. This technique is especially applicable to sales teams. A traditional sales meeting goes like this: The sales manager announces that sales are down for the quarter and begins asking (note the perspective here), "What's wrong?"

The salespeople in attendance begin coming up with all sorts of reasons (excuses) for the poor performance. They blame the economy (everyone's favorite whipping boy), government regulations, their health ("well, I was not feeling well, you know"), and whatever else they can think of to answer the disempowering question. After all, you can't not answer the boss's question, can you?

Since like attracts like, the entire meeting takes a downward turn. By the time the meeting is over, everyone is depressed as they head back to their desks. How likely are they to have a productive day of selling?

On the other hand, by using the value-finding approach, the team will begin discovering more and more things that *are* working. The conversation will remain positive, and people will begin coming up with creative solutions to the problem at hand.

Rather than following the typical meeting format and sitting around talking about all the problems and all the things going wrong, including the economy — an exercise that does a little more than suck the energy out of everyone present — ask the question, "What's working?," and you will create a new powerful, positive, upbeat dynamic, which will lead to more of the same. This is the first in a series of questions that I use with my business coaching and consulting clients as well as in my own business. It has proven, over a ten-year period, to be an invaluable tool for growing not only my clients' businesses but also my own.

I am not suggesting you ignore problems, just that you minimize their impact and never, ever allow them to set the tone of a meeting. If I want to explore what's wrong or not working, I can find endless reasons (excuses). But as a manager or business owner do you really care why sales are down, or do you want to change things?

Assuming that you would rather change the situation, where is the payoff in studying the problem? By identifying what is working, and employing other value-finding questions, you will learn what actions and activities are succeeding, and from there, you will be in a position to do more of what is actually working in order to grow your revenue.

By asking the "What's working?" question, you will stop spending time on low-value, low-return actions and concentrate your efforts where you are already succeeding.

By the way, this practice is critically important but rarely used when businesses evaluate their advertising. Too many business owners continue to buy worthless advertising simply because it's "what we've always done." If you measure your advertising against the "What's working?" yardstick, you may be surprised at what you learn.

The good news is that you can stop wasting money on what's not working and invest more in the activities and the media that are bringing you results. The net result of this is a big "cha-ching."

I can personally attest to the effectiveness of this technique. Each Monday morning my wife, Georgia, and I do this exercise for my business. To be perfectly honest, there are days when the list of what is working is pretty short; however, as a result of focusing on what is working, no matter how sparse, we align with the power of the law of attraction. Sometimes, even before the end of the day, we can add to this list since new opportunities come into our lives.

Whenever you find yourself stuck or feeling down about a situation, employ this simple technique and watch your circumstances improve.

24. *Learn to Deal with Difficult People*

No matter how nice a person you may be or how easy you think you are to get along with, in any organization there will be people who, for whatever reason, do not like you. There are people in many companies who just seem not to like anyone, for that matter.

No one says you have to like all your coworkers; however, you do still have to work with them. Sometimes this means having to work closely with people you'd just as soon not even be in the same room with. While you do not have to like your coworkers, you all have a job to do and are expected to do it. You have to find a way to get along, or the tension may become a detriment to the entire organization.

A concept I learned many years ago is "principles before personalities." I learned this in a recovery program, a situation in which someone I did not particularly like might just be the person to say something that could save my life.

In the context of your work environment the idea still holds true. While what a coworker says or does may not be lifesaving, it may well be what you need to hear to successfully complete a job, and it could be the difference between career advancement and termination. It is therefore imperative that you develop ways of dealing with people you'd just as soon avoid all together.

One of the best ways of learning to work with people, regardless of their personalities (or lack thereof), is always to treat them with respect. No matter what you may think of another person, he or she deserves respect. We all do.

Another practice is to look for what you like about people with whom you don't resonate. There is always something. Just as you can focus on what's working in a situation, as described above, you can always look for, and find, the good in another person. Does he handle his job well? Is she particularly good at a specific task? Look beneath the surface of an abrasive personality and see if you can find the real person. We are all human beings, and we all have at least the potential to be great.

Often when a person is difficult to get along with, there is an underlying cause. Many times they do not like themselves and reflect that to everyone they meet. Often, trying to see a situation from the other person's perspective can enable you to better understand their position.

To make working and communicating with people you do not get along with easier, focus on what you have in common rather than on your differences. For example, if you notice that a colleague likes old movies, as do you, ask him about his favorite old film. This will establish a topic you can both relate to and make working together easier. You may even be surprised to learn that you actually like your coworker!

Often if you take the time to get to know those difficult coworkers, you will find that they are decent, kind people who perhaps were simply shy and only appeared unfriendly. Learn to listen. Often all someone wants is to be heard. We all want to be recognized as human beings, and, given the opportunity, we can all learn to connect with one another as people, putting aside our differences and learning to work for the common good.

If you want to be happier and more effective at work, learn to set aside personalities and focus on the task at hand while at the same time treating everyone you encounter, in and out of work, with respect.

25. *Make Decisions Quickly*

A young Napoleon Hill stood before the steel mogul Andrew Carnegie, wondering why he had been summoned to meet with one of the richest men in the world. Carnegie, the sly old Scotsman, told the young, ambitious Hill that he had an assignment that might interest him. He went on to explain that he wanted Hill to interview the most successful men in America and learn why they were so successful.

He said it would take about twenty years to do this and, holding true to form, said he was not going to pay Hill for the work but would provide introductions to whomever he needed to meet. And, by the way, he wanted Hill's answer in sixty seconds.

What would you have done?

Hill thought about the offer for a few seconds and said yes, at which point Carnegie revealed the stopwatch he was holding behind his back. He was timing how long it took Hill to decide. Had Hill taken too long, Carnegie would have withdrawn the offer. Hill made a life-altering decision that would, over time, change the fortunes of millions of people — and he did it in less than a minute!

The result of Hill's work was, of course, the landmark book *Think and Grow Rich*, a book that is credited for creating more self-made millionaires than any other.

If you study successful people from all walks of life, you will find that they make decisions quickly and rarely change their mind once the decision is made. Too many people agonize over decisions, even small ones, and are quick to change at the first sign of a problem. The inability to act quickly has cost many a person the chance of a lifetime.

If you want to be more successful and as a result happier, cultivate the habit of making decisions quickly. This does not mean, however, that you should go off half-cocked. When faced with a decision, gather all the information available. If possible, talk it over with a trusted adviser, coach, or mentor. Pray and meditate about it, and then, once you've done all you can, make your decision.

Having made your decision, take whatever appropriate action is indicated, immediately. As I've said, the Universe likes speed.

Will every decision you make be the right one? Probably not; however, if you've evaluated the possible choices to the best of your ability, listened to wise counsel, and followed your intuition, the likelihood that you will make the right decision will be greatly increased.

26. *Get in Motion*

I learned one of the best phrases for making myself feel better at a Tony Robbins seminar more than two decades ago: "Motion equals emotion."

If you are feeling down or mildly depressed, the quickest way to change how you feel is to start moving. Of course, it goes without saying that if you are feeling depressed for a period of time you should seek professional medical help. It is not my intention to make light of a serious condition; however, what most of us experience from time to time is a feeling of "less-than-great," not clinical depression.

You've probably heard of the mind-body connection and may know about the emerging field of mind-body medicine. Science has been discovering just how big a part our mind plays in our physical health. Psychoneuroimmunology (the study of the interaction between psychological processes and the immune system) is one of the most exciting fields in medicine today and offers new insights into ways we can stay healthy.

Here is an exercise that demonstrates this principle of motion equaling emotion. Pretend for a moment that you are depressed. Sit the way you would if you were feeling down. Tell yourself what you might say if you were depressed. Hold your head the way you would if you were depressed. What would your facial expression look like?

How do you feel? I'm guessing you're starting to feel pretty lousy. Your mental and emotional states are now in sync with your physiology. The way you are holding your body and what you are saying to yourself are causing you to feel depressed.

Fortunately, the opposite is also true. Sit the way you would if you felt fantastic, if everything in your life were ideal, and you were having an amazing day. You're probably sitting up straight and tall, with a big grin on your face, right?

The next time you're out in public, look at the people around you. Take note of how they are carrying themselves. You can usually tell how they're feeling just by observing their posture and facial expressions.

The next time you're feeling a little low, get up and start moving. Go for a walk, even if it's just around your office or the building you work in. Imagine you are feeling unstoppable. What would your self-talk be? How would you be carrying yourself? What would your facial expression be?

I realize this may sound simple but, believe me, it works. Studies have been done with depressed people in mental hospitals that found that something as simple as having people walk around smiling for a while lowered incidents of mood swings and lessened the need for medication.

Our minds and bodies are inextricably linked. You cannot alter one without affecting the other. Knowing this and developing ways to use this dynamic to your benefit puts you more in control of how you feel.

It's interesting to note that one of the indicators of mental wellness is how much control we feel we have over our lives and our environment. Learning ways to improve how you feel goes a long way toward feeling more in control of your life.

27. *Gauge Your Happiness*

D r. Wayne Dyer was quoted as saying, "There is no way to happiness; happiness is the way." This belief is a key to being happier, whether at work or in your personal life.

The way to be happier is to simply be happy. Find the things that make you happy, and do them. Take charge of your thoughts and dwell only on the ones that make you feel good.

Being the author of both *Handbook to a Happier Life* and *52 Ways to a Happier Life*, I am considered an authority on the subject of happiness and have been asked numerous times, during media interviews, why people are not happier, especially at work.

This has become one of my favorite interview questions because the answer is so obvious, at least to me. One of the main reasons that more people are not happier at work is simply that they have not taken the time to ask themselves what makes them happy.

Instead, many people choose to focus on what's wrong with their job or on what they perceive as problems, rather than on what they appreciate. Finding reasons to feel appreciation in your every-day life is one of the fastest ways to feel happier.

Another way to feel better about yourself is to do something for another person. Most people report feeling happier when help-ing a fellow human being, and studies have shown that volunteering increases our happiness levels as well as our overall health. And, of course, getting involved in volunteering will help you to feel better, but you will be helping your community as well.

I realize this may sound like an oversimplification, but it's true. We are not taught to identify the activities, attitudes, and actions that add to our happiness. Instead it is all left to chance.

We are brainwashed by the media to believe that in order to be happy we must achieve a certain level of professional success, usually defined by someone else. While there is nothing wrong with wanting to excel, career success alone will not make you happy. This becomes obvious when one looks at the number of very successful but unhappy people in our society.

This was one of those lessons that I had to learn the hard way. Only after I had lost almost all my stuff did I understand that happiness was something I was free to choose at any time.

Fortunately, I was able to acquire more material possessions and can enjoy them without being attached to them. There is nothing wrong with wanting nice things, as long as you understand that it's just "stuff" and will not make you feel better for more than a fleeting moment.

Take the time to identify the thoughts, experiences, activities, and conditions that add to your happiness and find ways to add more of them to your life. Think about what makes you happy. Look for ways to feel happier. The easiest and best way to accomplish this is to look for things to be grateful for.

Since unhappiness is usually connected to feelings of self-pity, and it is impossible to be in a state of gratitude and self-pity at the same time, when you focus on those things you are grateful for, you automatically begin to feel happier.

28. *Be Exceptional*

Whether you're an entry-level intern, an account executive, a senior VP, or the CEO, I have a news flash for you — "good enough" is no longer good enough.

In the twenty-first-century workplace, with its fierce global competition and the abundance of well-qualified people vying for jobs, what was once considered acceptable — that is, "good" — no longer works. If you want to excel in your career, you'll need to raise your standards. You'll need to become exceptional.

Look around. The hugely successful companies are performing in an exceptional manner. Apple immediately comes to mind, especially since I've been a diehard Mac user and Apple fan for many years.

One of the things that has made Apple great is the elegance of their products, as anyone who has ever used them knows. The late Steve Jobs insisted on designing elegant, easy-to-use goods. At a time when all the emphasis was on technology, Apple designed user-friendly products that people enjoyed. Their user base became missionaries, singing Apple's praises to anyone who'd listen.

Many other companies have done the same and distinguished themselves in the marketplace by offering superior products and services. Zappos took over the online shoe business in just such a manner, as did Amazon with books and more.

In food service, companies such as Panera Bread and Starbucks have raised the bar, forcing their competitors to do better. Even McDonalds now offers premium coffee and is making a sincere attempt to offer healthier food choices.

In the hotel industry, the difference between a good hotel and a great one is often simply a matter of offering turndown service and placing mints on the pillows.

What can you do to raise the bar for yourself and add more value to your company? One way is to consistently challenge yourself by asking, "How might I improve this process?" or, "What can we do to deliver even better service?"

If you continue to raise the bar, for yourself and your organization, not only will you be a more valuable employee to your company or, if you're an entrepreneur, more successful in your own business but you'll also have more fun in the process. We typically derive more pleasure from those things we are good at.

29. *Drink Water*

Recently a chiropractor friend of mine posted on Facebook that the majority of new patients he sees are suffering from dehydration, the root cause of occasional and even chronic back pain. This assessment, something I've heard from several other chiropractors I've known over the years, is one of the easiest conditions to remedy. Simply drink more water.

Unfortunately most people drink very little pure water, a practice that leads not only to aches and pains but to a host of other issues as well, including digestive problems.

If you've ever been on a diet or joined a weight-loss program, you know that they all suggest drinking eight to ten glasses of water a day. Soda does not count, nor does coffee or tea. Your body perceives these as food, not water.

When you consider that our bodies are made up of approximately 60 percent water, according to the *Anatomy and Physiology for Nurses*, it becomes obvious that we need to drink more of it. Obesity, by the way, can decrease this amount to about 45 percent.

You can do several things to ensure you are getting enough water. For starters, make a practice of drinking a large glass of water first thing in the morning. Putting a piece of fresh lemon in it has the added benefit of helping to detox your liver.

Make a habit of keeping a glass or bottle of water near your work area and sip it throughout the day. My colleague Jack Canfield, the success guru, said that he has his assistant place eight bottles of water on his desk each morning and does not leave his office for the day until he's drunk them all.

A tip I learned back in the days when I smoked and drank alcohol was to drink a large glass of water with every cocktail I imbibed. I believe this is one of the reasons that I managed to avoid having any liver problems. Doing so also reduces the aftereffects of the hangover brought on by your overindulgence. While I'm not suggesting you consume alcohol, if you do, this will lessen the negative effects of the alcohol.

An Internet search for *water* and *dehydration* turns up a wealth of health-related results. Suffice it to say that dehydration is dangerous, affecting many of your bodily functions, and can lead to serious illness, so drinking plenty of water is more than just a nice idea.

How much pure water are you drinking each day? What could you do to improve this?

30. *Don't Gossip*

If there's one topic necessary in a book about the workplace, it's gossip. For whatever reason, offices, stores, factories, and almost every other location where people gather to work are riddled with people who seem to have nothing better to do than gossip about their coworkers.

While gossiping has always been portrayed in movies and television shows as a "woman's thing," the truth is that men are just as guilty of engaging in this pointless and destructive habit.

Gossip can ruin working relationships and undermine the most productive businesses. It can lower morale, create a difficult work environment, and even cause good people to leave the company.

Spreading gossip not only harms the reputation of the person it is directed toward but also is destructive to the person spreading it. While I'll never totally understand why people gossip, I believe it has to do with their lack of self-esteem and a feeling that since there's nothing of consequence going on in their own lives, they may as well trash-talk other people.

My suggestion regarding gossip is simple — don't do it! Refuse to engage in gossip, and avoid being around those who seem to make it their life's mission. The last thing you want is to become known as someone who spreads gossip about your coworkers, or for that matter, anyone else.

What if you're the target of the gossip? If someone is gossiping about you, take the person aside and talk privately with him. Explain to him, as calmly as possible, that you will not tolerate his spreading false and hurtful rumors about you. Let him know, in no uncertain terms, that if it continues you will bring the problem to management. And, if it does continue, do so.

If you hear a coworker spreading gossip about someone else, let that person know you're not interested in hearing such things, and go about your own business.

Of course, it goes without saying that gossiping is one of the worst career moves you can make. Not only does it make people not want to be around you, but once top management learns of it, it will block your possible advancement within the organization.

How do you deal with people who gossip at your job?

31. *Take Ownership of Your Work*

One practice that has served me well throughout my working life is taking ownership of whatever job I held or task I was performing.

This trait, instilled in me at a young age, is responsible for much of the success I've achieved thus far. From my first real job as a teenager busing tables in a restaurant, to my current role as an author, speaker, and trainer, this practice has helped me do the very best job I am capable of every time.

By taking ownership you are, in effect, signing your work, and, as such, you are more inclined to do your best. Many companies realize that empowering their employees and enabling them to take ownership of their job result in enhanced performance. When we feel this kind of pride, whether it's of a job or our home, we are more likely to pay attention to whatever it is we're taking ownership of.

If you were the owner of your company and tasked with the job you're doing, how would you approach the work? What would you do differently? Would you cut corners just to get it done and call it a day? Probably not. You'd be more likely to do your very best and take pride in your accomplishments.

Here's something to consider: in terms of your area of responsibility, *you* are the owner of your job. How you perform at work reflects the type of individual you are, so make a habit of doing the best job you can at all times.

When you see something that needs to be done, do it. Don't wait for someone to tell you it needs to be addressed. Just take the initiative and act. When a situation arises that needs attention or requires that a decision be made, if it is within the realm of your responsibility, handle it. Make the decision.

We've all seen people at our jobs who, when the slightest problem occurs, look for someone to tell them what to do. These are often lower-level employees who, unfortunately, rarely rise above their level due to their lack of initiative. They are the ones who are afraid that if they make a decision they might be blamed if something goes wrong.

On the surface this may seem like a logical thing to do; however, in practice it demonstrates an inability to lead. Leaders willingly risk making a decision and take full responsibility for its outcome. Are they always right? Of course not, but, as some wise person once said, you only have to be right most of the time to succeed.

Of course, there will be times when you'll want to take a problem to your superior, but the more day-to-day issues that you handle yourself, the more likely it is that your natural leadership ability will be recognized and that you will rise within the organization.

My wife, Georgia, rose to an executive position in a giant telecommunications company by being willing to step up and make decisions. She said, "I'd rather ask forgiveness than permission."

32. *Cultivate Good Habits*

A habit is something we do over and over again until it becomes automatic. There are productive habits, those that support us and help us progress toward the life we want, and then there are destructive habits, those that take us farther away from what we want.

Some of our good habits we learned at a very young age, and they still support us. Things like brushing our teeth, taking regular baths and showers, and engaging in other personal-hygiene activities have become automatic.

If you examine your habits, you may be surprised to learn that many of the ones you'd like to change were also learned at a very young age. The tendency to eat foods high in sugar content was probably created when you were a child. Now, as an adult, instead of taking the time to go to the company cafeteria for a healthy meal, you grab a candy bar or some equally low-nutrition food from the vending machine in the hallway. You tell yourself you're too busy to take the time to eat when in reality your productivity will be lessened because of the unhealthy lunch you had. Eating junk food in the workplace is often the cause of people's afternoon slumps, not to mention a leading contributor to our current obesity epidemic.

Sometimes we need to motivate ourselves to take a particular action for a certain period of time until it becomes a habit. It takes about three to four weeks to instill a new habit in ourselves. For me, exercising was something I had to push myself to do for the first few months. Now I feel as though I've missed something if I do not get to the health club regularly. Allow yourself sufficient time to learn a new habit. Don't quit before the miracle happens.

Activity Steps: Listing Your Habits

- Make a list of four or five habits that support your goals. In what ways might you expand on them?
- Make a list of four or five habits that are not supporting you. In what ways might you begin to replace them with more empowering and supportive ones?

33. *Identify Your Beliefs*

Beliefs are one of my favorite subjects. If there is one thing that keeps most people from having everything they want in their lives, it is what they believe about themselves, their abilities, and the world they live in. Everything you do and everything you have accomplished or ever will accomplish is governed by your beliefs.

Where Do Beliefs Come From?

A belief, quite simply, is something you have told yourself over and over throughout your life. Beliefs start at a young age. If we try something for the first time and we fail, we label ourselves a failure. For example, if at the age of ten or twelve, I attempted to play basketball but because of my age and size was not yet very good at it, I may have created a belief in my mind that I will never be able to play basketball. This may not have been true, because beliefs rarely are.

A more common example is the person who once tried starting her own business but was not successful. She created a belief that she was not meant to be in business, and therefore she never tried it again. This is really sad when you consider that almost every successful businessperson has experienced many failures. The difference is in the way they view the experience and the beliefs they create from them. One person may see a business failure as a sign that he cannot be a successful business owner, while another will only view it as a temporary setback and turn it into a learning experience.

Other People's Beliefs

One of my favorite belief stories comes from what happened to me several years ago when I started a publication for small-business owners. I felt there was a need for a local publication that would provide small-business owners with information to help them in their businesses, and I decided to go for it. Quite honestly, I did not have a lot of knowledge about or experience in publishing a magazine, but I knew enough to get started and I trusted my instincts. I had placed an ad in our local newspaper for a salesperson to help with selling the advertising, and I interviewed several people.

The day after the first issue was published, one of the people I had interviewed called me. He was an advertising salesperson for a weekly newspaper and, while he wished me well, he had decided not to change jobs. We had spoken in early June and it was now the first week of September. The premier issue was out in time for Labor Day, as I had promised the advertisers. The man asked, "How did you do it?" I replied, "How did I do what?" He said, "How did you publish this magazine so quickly? It was only two months ago, and you were just getting started." I thought for a moment and told the man the truth: I had no idea how long it was supposed to take to publish a magazine. I had no beliefs about the time needed. He told me that it takes at least six months to bring out a new publication. But this was not a fact. It was merely his belief.

Because of my inexperience I had no such belief. I published the magazine within two months. Don't let someone else's beliefs stand in the way of your success.

How Beliefs Determine Results

Let's take a closer look at how our beliefs determine our results. Most people would agree that we human beings have unlimited potential. Why, then, do we not see this borne out in our accomplishments? This is where beliefs come into play. The result you produce is determined by the actions you take. The problem is, most of us have a limiting belief in our ability to accomplish a particular task. We tap into only a small portion of our potential, take limited action, and produce a poor result.

An example of this principle is the secretary who tries learning the company's new computer system but then gives up, because he believes he cannot successfully learn new technology. Or the salesperson who makes a weak attempt at making sales calls before deciding that the profession is not for her and moving on to yet another job. In reality, her limiting belief in her ability to succeed in sales is what caused her to take such weak action in the first place. If you interview top salespeople in any organization, you'll find that they all learned to overcome any beliefs that may have been standing in the way of their success.

Fortunately, the opposite is also true. If you develop a belief that you can do whatever you set your mind to, you will tap into your limitless potential, take effective action, and produce greater results. My favorite examples of this principle are the countless stories of people who've overcome seemingly insurmountable obstacles to accomplish their dreams.

One such person is Sara Blakely, founder of the hugely successful women's accessory brand Spanx. Her father instilled in her a belief that failure was simply part of the process of success, not something to be feared. This strongly held empowering belief enabled Blakely to make her mark on the hosiery industry and become the youngest female billionaire in US history.

Identifying Your Limiting Beliefs

If you want to identify your limiting beliefs, pay attention to what you say about your ability in a particular area. For example, if you are having trouble making sales, you'll likely hear yourself say something like, "I can't make more sales because..." Whatever comes after the word *because* is usually your limiting belief.

You'll hear people say things like, "I can't get ahead in my company because I'm not good at managing people." This, of course is not true; it's simply a belief. Good managers are not born good. They learn how to manage people.

You owe it to yourself to identify and correct the beliefs that are standing in the way of your success. One way to do this is to simply question the belief. Ask yourself if your belief is really true or something you were told by someone else. Chances are it's not true. Once you've questioned the belief, you've begun to weaken its hold over you.

There are many other ways to undo limiting beliefs, from creating affirmations that counter the belief to using techniques such as Emotional Freedom Technique (EFT) or some other type of therapy designed to change behavioral patterns.

Once you've started to break down your limiting beliefs, you'll want to begin creating new, empowering ones to take their place. One technique I particularly like I learned from Michael Losier, author of the book *Law of Attraction*. As a way to help your subconscious accept a new affirmation, he suggests beginning with the words "I'm in the process of...," followed by your new affirmation. For example, if you wish to become a better salesperson you might say, "I'm in the process of becoming the top salesperson in the company."

Activity Steps: Identifying Your Beliefs

- Make a list of three or four beliefs that are preventing you from becoming the person you want to be.
- Next, create an affirmation that contradicts each of these beliefs and is more in alignment with who you want to be.

As you question your limiting beliefs and replace them with more empowering ones, they will begin to break down and, after a while, will no longer be standing in the way of your ideal life.

34. Make Personal Development Part of Your Daily Routine

B usiness guru Brian Tracy once commented that whenever he interviewed a prospective employee, one of the first questions he would ask was, "What's the last self-help book you read?" I'm guessing that the answer had a lot to do with how long the rest of the interview would last and with the candidate's chances of being hired.

With finding good jobs becoming more difficult every day, this is a question worth considering. Maybe you're asking yourself why anyone, especially a prospective employer, would care what you read. From where I sit, it's quite simple. If you're not interested in your personal growth and professional development, are you really someone I want representing my company?

It's a fact that many successful people make a habit out of reading and listening to personal-development information. Years ago, audio program producer Nightingale-Conant conducted a survey of their customers and asked what value, in dollars, they would place on having listened to one of the company's programs. The average value people placed on having listened to personal-development programs was $180,000.

Years ago my friend John, a car salesman, increased his income by 15 percent during one of the worst automotive slumps in history. The only thing he changed was that he began a practice of reading self-help books for fifteen to twenty minutes each day before going to work.

Millionaire network marketers teach their people to read each day as a way to remain motivated. The people who are successful in that industry are the ones who follow that advice.

Sadly, most people have not read a book since they left school, and a third of the population in the United States, according to a *Huffington Post*/US government poll in September 2013, have not read a book in a year. In Korea, in 2006 more money was spent on cigarettes than on books.

Joe Girard wrote the book *How to Sell Anything to Anybody* about how he became the number one car salesman in the world. It amazes me that so few of the car salespeople I meet have read it.

I have watched my life change for the better in direct proportion to how much I was reading and listening to each day. To this day, if I start to feel less than great it's usually because I have not been keeping up my practice of ongoing personal development.

Lots of great books have been published, and more are being released each week. Of course, I'd prefer you start with one of mine, but whatever you choose, make sure it's something that will nurture your spirit and help you maintain a positive outlook.

Make personal development a part of your daily routine, and you will learn, as I did, that it is one of the secrets to a happier, more successful life.

35. Remember That This Too Shall Pass

Mike was known as "Iron Mike" to his friends, not so much because he was a tough guy but because he had been an iron worker and was old-school, blue-collar, working-class Staten Island Irish, much like the members of my own family. Mike had been a serious drinker for many years. Oh, yeah, and he was tough too.

What I remember most about him, aside from his always outstretched hand and his readiness to welcome any newcomer to the fellowship we were both members of, was his response whenever someone said, "This too shall pass." "Yeah," Mike would bellow, "The good passes, the bad passes, and then you pass."

Whatever is happening in your life — the good and the not-so-good — will pass as surely as day passes into night. If you're going through a difficult period right now, hang tight; it will pass. Similarly, that fantastic feeling you're having right now will also pass. It's the natural ebb and flow of life.

You remember life. It's that thing that John Lennon said happens while we're busy making other plans.

My favorite lesson for getting through challenges comes from nature. Everything in nature survives by being in the flow of life, not by trying to resist it. Everything — from the trees growing along the California coast, which withstand the high winds and rough seas of the Pacific Ocean, to the coral in the Great Barrier Reef in Australia — thrives by living in harmony with the world around it.

Whatever is going on in your life right now, especially if it's challenging, go with the flow. Ride the waves of the changes that are taking place the way a surfer rides ocean waves. Just go with the ebb and flow of your life. And remember, this too shall pass.

36. *Tell a Different Story*

I often receive email from people in various parts of the world who have read one of my books or listened to an audio or video course I've recorded. Many of them ask what they can do to improve their circumstances. While this is quite natural, considering the work I do, I find it troubling that, in almost every case, the person goes on and on about "the way things are." What they, and many others, are doing is reinforcing the situation by telling the same story over and over again. Unfortunately, it's a story about exactly what they don't want.

You can't keep telling the same story and expect conditions to change. If you want to improve your life, you must begin telling yourself a new story. The best thing you can do is to stop talking about the problem.

Yes, conditions at many jobs can be trying; however, continuing to talk about them and feeling victimized does nothing more than give energy to the problem. Whether you're trying to increase sales, grow your business, or just have time to complete your work, the law of attraction is always at work.

All religious and spiritual teachings teach something similar to the statement in the Bible "As a man thinketh in his heart, so is he." We attract what we think about. Period. It's nonnegotiable. You cannot keep saying things such as "The economy is down, so sales are off" and expect things to magically change.

We must all learn to make our conversation be about what we do want rather than what we do not want. You must begin writing a new story about your job and your life. Start talking to yourself about how everything is getting better and better each day.

Learn to focus on what you do have, on what you are thankful for, however little that may be at this time, and on what is going right in your life.

Spend some time each day envisioning the life you want. Feel it with all your senses. If you're in sales, start seeing people eager to buy from you. Imagine a new story about how business is increasing. See yourself shaking hands with your new customer. Experience how great it feels to be so successful.

If there's a job you want, begin by imagining yourself working in this ideal career, enjoying your work and feeling appreciated. Of course, don't stop there. We have an active role to play in our lives, so after you envision the life you want, get up and do something to move toward it, however small the first step may seem at the moment.

If you want to start or grow a business, instead of looking at obstacles, however real they may seem, start looking for ways you can provide service. When you find ways to serve your community, your fellow human beings, and the world at large, you will begin to see ways in which you can earn money. It's never the other way around.

I know of no successful people who first began by looking for ways to make money. Financial abundance is always the result of doing something that provides value in the world.

Begin now writing the story of your new life. Write it down, act it out, see it, feel it, and start moving toward it. As the title of one of my other books reminds us *What Are You Waiting For? It's Your Life.*

37. *Model the Success You Desire*

I f you allow it and are open to it, you can learn from everyone you meet. Depending on the encounter, either you can learn how to achieve the results you want, or, as is in the case of undesirable encounters, you can learn what not to do. Both lessons can be valuable.

Over the years I've made a practice of studying people who have achieved something I'd like to accomplish. Whether in health, fitness, business, or even relationships, if I want to achieve a particular result, I can find someone who achieved it and learn to do what they did. This idea, known as modeling, is a simple, powerful way to increase performance in any area of your career or personal life and is a strategy that can be used by anyone.

Simply find someone who is a achieving the kind of results you'd like in a given area and learn what she does and how she does it. If possible, meet with her personally and ask for her help. You could interview a top producer in your company, for example, and learn what she did. Then simply follow in her footsteps.

If you were doing this in sales, for example, one of the things you would model is the person's strategy — specifically, what she does and how she does it. You would also elicit her thought processes as best you can.

In business one essential thing you want to model from a successful person is his beliefs. This, by the way, is one reason you want to read and watch biographies of the successful people you want to emulate — it will give you fresh perspectives and help you develop new, more empowering beliefs.

If you're in sales, modeling the beliefs and strategies of top people will give you new ideas about your job. I guarantee that the salesperson in your company who earns ten times the average does not work ten times harder. Rather, he is operating from a different set of beliefs and guiding principles, using different strategies, and taking different actions.

If at all possible, invite the top seller in your company for coffee or to lunch and ask him for suggestions. Most of the successful people I know are only too happy to share ideas, since doing so deepens their own understanding and gives them new insights.

Modeling can be a great boon to your personal and business success. Learning from others who have achieved what you want can cut years off your learning curve and propel you toward your success faster than if you did it on your own. Remember, success is a team sport. No one, and I mean no one, does it alone.

When I was a beginning writer, I attended seminars for authors and publishers, and I listened to audio recordings of people who had succeeded in selling their books. Whatever you want to achieve, in any area of your life or business, finding role models to learn from is one of the wisest things you can do for your own success.

Look over your top goals and determine who has achieved success in that area and might be able to help you. If you don't know anyone personally, you can usually find a book written by someone who has done what it is you're working on. You can listen to podcasts, audiobooks, and webinars. You can watch videos and attend seminars. You may want to join an industry association in your field.

Associations are known for having professional education, and some even offer mentoring programs from more seasoned members.

It's an accepted fact that people who do their jobs well are happier overall than those who struggle. It stands to reason that we enjoy what we do well, so by becoming the best you can at whatever you do, you will be increasing your happiness, not to mention improving your standing at work.

By making modeling part of your personal-development strategy you will achieve greater results faster than ever before.

38. *Define Your Success*

Some people equate success with having a lot of money. While there's nothing wrong with money, and we all need it (as we'll discuss below), it alone will not make you feel successful. Too many people spend their lives chasing after money, only to find that it isn't making them happy. Some have even lost everything in their obsessive quest for more dollars, yen, rubles, and pesos.

Others believe that having strong family and community connections results in feeling successful. Of course, while these ties are an important component of a successful life, they too are not all there is.

Personal-development legend Earl Nightingale defined success as "the progressive realization of a worthy ideal." Again, though this is an important part of a successful life and is certainly a great compass for deciding where to direct your efforts, it is also not all there is.

In my opinion, creating and enjoying a successful life is a combination of balancing several key areas. Cultivating a deep spiritual connection to your Creator is, in my opinion, essential for achieving a truly successful life. It is the glue that holds the rest together. Having loving relationships and a strong connection to your friends and community certainly contributes greatly to your feeling more successful. Meaningful work — doing something that you deem worth devoting your time to — is another key.

Whatever you spend your time doing, ask yourself if it's worth the price you're paying, namely, your life. If it is, terrific. Keep doing it. If not, what can you do to change it? How might you spend more of your time doing the things you feel are important and less time doing things that are not?

An obvious key to a successful life is good health, although judging from the way people ignore it, you'd think otherwise. We all need a certain amount of energy to enjoy our life's pursuits, and we certainly want to remain free of illness and disease.

Developing and maintaining a healthy lifestyle — complete with a healthy diet, a reasonable amount of exercise, and regular health checkups — will go a long way to bolstering your well-being. The increased energy you will enjoy as a result will help you in your quest for greater success in all areas of your life.

The last, but no less important, area to consider is financial wellness. In order to feel successful and have a full life, we need money. While most people would agree that money is not all there is, it is necessary for many of life's pleasures.

You can have all the love there is, but your banker is not going to take it as your mortgage payment. And your cable company doesn't want to hear about your fantastic health when the bill is due. Yes, money is important.

One of the best ways to ensure financial health and security is to develop more than one stream of income, whether you're an employee or you work for yourself. Of course, living within your means and not taking on unnecessary debt is important as well, as is taking the time to learn about investing and paying close attention to your finances.

Balancing all these different parts of your life can be tricky. This is why I suggest creating an overall vision for the life you want and setting measurable goals based on that vision. It has been said that "what gets measured, gets done."

Taking the time to define what success means to you and then tracking your activities will reward you with a life beyond anything you could have expected.

You deserve a successful life filled with all the joy, love, and happiness you desire. Accepting less is shortchanging yourself.

What simple step will you take today to begin to define and create your amazing success?

39. *Don't Get Derailed*

Years ago I had the pleasure of following the PGA professional golf tour and getting to know some of the top pros of the day. At the time, I was producing a series of videotaped golf lessons, which, unfortunately, was just a little ahead of its time. To compound the problem, I was also in the midst of self-destructing, so the project never got off the ground.

I did, however, spend a season traveling to the top tournaments and met and worked with some great pro golfers, such as Frank Beard, Al Geiberger, Bobby Nichols, and Dave Stockton. I had the pleasure of spending several hours talking with Julie Burroughs, considered one of the nicest people in the sport at the time.

What I observed among these superstars was that, in addition to being dedicated to the game and having the discipline to keep practicing even after playing a round, they had the unique ability to quickly recover from a bad shot. They did not let a poor shot carry over to the next hole. This is part of what makes them winners.

One evening I was talking with Frank Beard at dinner. He was explaining that one of the traits that made Al Geiberger a great golfer was his ability to focus all his attention on the task at hand. He didn't lament the missed shot on a previous hole, instead putting total effort into hitting the shot in front of him.

By the way, Geiberger won eleven times on the PGA Tour and

ten times on the Champions Tour; however, he is best known as the first person to shoot a "mythical" 59 in a major tournament, the Danny Thomas Memphis Classic on June 10, 1977.

Similarly, a runner who trips on a pothole while running a race does not stop and stand there looking at the hole. Instead, she gets up and gets back in the race.

These lessons from the world of sports can be applied to your career and other parts of your life. What do you do when you make a mistake? Do you replay the experience over and over again in your mind, berating yourself for your error? Or do you behave more like the pro athletes, learning what you can from the experience, letting it go, and getting on with your life?

We all have failed outcomes, especially in business. I could go on, in great detail, about the lost opportunity with our golf video business, but the truth is, (no pun intended) I dropped the ball.

You're going to make mistakes — unless, of course, you never attempt anything. Assuming you do take some action, you will mess up. The best thing you can do is learn something from your mistake and move on.

I personally do not know of anyone who has achieved high levels of success without experiencing setbacks, problems, and even complete failures. The difference between the champions and the weekend "duffers" is that champions continue on, even in the face of adversity.

Resolve now not to let your setbacks derail your success. Be like the professional golfers and "play the shot in front of you."

40. *Begin Now*

We've all said it at one time or another. "Someday I'll...go back to school, ask for a raise, improve my skills so I can be promoted, find a new job, start saving for our future."

What is your version of "Someday I'll...?"

Well, my friend, let me be the first to inform you that today is that someday you've been waiting for.

A quotation that was popular in the 1960s reminded us that "today is the first day of the rest of your life." This quote could be seen on T-shirts, posters, and signs everywhere. (I'm not sure who actually stated it, but it's been attributed to Bob Dylan.)

There will never be a better time to begin whatever project you've been wanting to undertake. The reason is simple. Now is the only time there is and the only time there ever will be. As the title of one of my other books reminds us, *What Are You Waiting For? It's Your Life*.

We all tend to use the "Someday I'll..." excuse as a way to delude ourselves into believing that we will, one day soon, study for the promotion test or go back to school, when, in fact, all we're doing is procrastinating — probably out of a fear of not succeeding. We do things for basically one of two reasons: we either want to gain pleasure or avoid pain. That's it, folks. Everything we do breaks down to one or, more likely, a combination of these two emotional states.

So how do you change this dynamic? The best way to motivate yourself is quite simple. Take control of what is sometimes referred to as the "carrot and the stick"— the perceived pain and pleasure connected to your action. Let's say, for example, that you want to complete your education. What will it mean for your career and overall happiness if you do? Imagine how great it will feel. What will you gain in terms of your earning ability and future work prospects? How will you feel? This is the "carrot," the pleasure motivator. On the other side of the equation, because I feel they're both useful at different times, is the "stick," or pain motivator. Imagine what you would be missing out on if you didn't complete your education.

When I did this assessment for my health and fitness it was easy to gain leverage. One morning I sat quietly, eyes closed, and projected out twenty years. I then imagined what my life would be like if I continued to eat unhealthy food and to ignore physical exercise.

Believe me when I tell you that what I saw scared me. I realized that if I didn't change my habits, I was looking at a depressing future. I then imagined how I would feel not only twenty years out but also in the immediate future . . . if I took action immediately.

I remember that day as if it were yesterday, even though it was more than twenty years ago. After taking a few minutes to write in my journal the result of my carrot-and-stick exercise so I could refer to it and stay motivated, I got up, put on a pair of sneakers, and started an exercise program that I've pretty much stayed with since.

Sure, I may slack off since I'm only human, but I am always aware of my diet and exercise choices and have remained committed to my health since that day.

Whatever it is you want to do "someday," begin it today.

Activity Steps: Taking Action

Take a few minutes and write out your desire(s). Sit quietly and imagine that you took action and it's now ten or twenty years into the future. Then, answer the following questions in your journal.

- What are all the benefits you've enjoyed because you acted today?
- What have you been able to do because of this action?
- What has it meant to your family and community?

Next, do the reverse.

- What has the fact that you didn't take action cost you?
- What is it already costing you now? Chances are that your not doing something has some unpleasant consequence in the present as well.

I think you can guess the next step.

Begin!

For, as Goethe said, "Whatever you can do or dream you can, begin it. Boldness has genius, power and magic in it!"

41. *Let Go*

Do you have days like this too — days when you feel, well, confused?

I woke up one morning at about 3:30 AM, not my usual time. I was feeling, as I do from time to time, a little confused about what to do next, what path to take, what projects to focus on, and so on.

While each of us is living with different circumstances, and no one solution will fit everyone, I have learned some things over the years that can help at times like this.

The first thing I do, rather than running around like a crazy person and becoming even more confused, is to become quiet. I take time for meditation. This quiets my mind and allows me to focus my attention.

I then pray. I ask for guidance in making the correct choices and then, and here's the real power in this process, I give over the entire situation to the care of my Higher Power.

I've learned from experience that the phrase "let go and let God" is not just some clever saying but is, in fact, a powerful strategy that will resolve any situation. If you're facing a challenge, I suggest you use this technique and learn for yourself the amazing power in letting go and giving your problem to a power greater than yourself.

A lot of people have difficulty understanding how to let go. Many of us attempt to let go of something only to try to take back control a moment later. Someone once taught me that letting go of a troublesome issue is like mailing a letter. Once you put it into the mailbox, you have to completely let go of it if you are to mail it. It's the same with your challenge. You can't keep taking it back. Just let go of it for a time. Once you have more clarity, you can then take it up again and work through it.

This does not mean you give up or that there's nothing for you to do to affect the situation. Letting go, or surrendering a condition to your Higher Power, is not the same as doing nothing. There is always something for you to do. There's always a next step or small action for you to take.

Letting go is the same as opening yourself up to the guidance that is available to us all. It is releasing your attachment to the outcome and being willing to be led by a power greater than yourself. When you do this, in a relatively short time you will feel an impulse to take a certain action. Take that action, even though it may not be what you expected.

After my meditation and prayer time, I usually go for a walk. Physical activity and movement is a great way to change your perspective and engages many more of your senses. You can learn more about this in chapter 26.

A relaxing walk, one in which your mind can just drift and you can allow your senses to take in the world around you, is one of the best mind-body activities you can employ, especially when working through a confusing or challenging time.

In my case, after or even during my walk I'll get an idea or impulse to do something I had not thought of, and, more often than not, I will have found an answer to my challenge or learned a new way to approach it.

42. *Put the Excitement Back in Your Job*

D o you sometimes find yourself just going through the motions of your job? Has the excitement gone out of your daily routine?

Remember way back when you started your job? You were excited and enthusiastic about all your tasks. What went wrong? Where did the excitement and enthusiasm go? More important, how do you get them back?

If you're feeling this way, of course, it may be a signal that it is time for you to make some changes or to move on. On the other hand, maybe you just need to get back in touch with why you took the job in the first place.

If you are in your own business, it may not be possible to move on, so you'll need to learn ways to bring back the excitement. There is nothing more depressing than to see small-business owners (or employees) who have stopped enjoying their work. These are the people who sit in their stores or offices just waiting for the day when they can retire. They feel stuck, unable to get out. They have lost their zest for their work.

If you're one of these people just going through the motions, remember that your life is too important to let it slip by. Don't let yourself lead a life, as Thoreau said, "of quiet desperation."

So how can you bring back the zest? For starters, go back to your original business plan or personal journal and reread the reasons you embarked on this business or career in the first place. What were your goals? Are these reasons still valid? Do they still ring true for you today? If they do, sit quietly and get back in touch with your feelings from that time. Get the juices flowing again. Relive the experiences that led you to this place. Rekindle the flames.

If you have drifted from your original purpose, perhaps you need to rethink why you are doing the job you're doing now. In the case of your own business, maybe you need to change or modify your original direction. This could be as simple as offering a new product or service, something that gives you passion.

Perhaps you could open new markets or venture into exporting to get your juices going again. Do something that puts the joy back in your day. Paint your store! Change your tie! Perhaps all you need to do is delegate some of the tasks you dislike and concentrate on doing what you love.

Try this simple exercise. On a sheet of paper or in your journal, complete the following two sentences:

1. What I really enjoy about my work/business is that I _____.

   This could be that you have the opportunity to travel to interesting places or meet people or help others — whatever you enjoy most.
2. The real benefit to my customers from my work is _____.

I know a building contractor whose attitude toward his work changed when he stopped thinking of himself as simply a contractor and started realizing how he helped people turn their dreams into reality. This shift had a major impact on his self-esteem and, as a result, his income.

Sometimes I run across a store that still has one of the old signs that read "Through our doors pass some of the finest people in the world. Our customers." Maybe it's corny, but I can't help but feel special in a place like that.

If you are going to a job today just because you went there yesterday, you are in a danger zone. You deserve to be enthusiastic, excited, and even ecstatic about your livelihood. Sometimes you have to re-create that feeling.

Remember the words of the late Norman Vincent Peale, who said that what happens to us is not nearly as important as how we interpret what happens.

Work with passion!

43. *Remove the Obstacles Blocking Your Success*

Often the obstacle that's standing in our way is the result of our asking ourselves the wrong question. Simply changing the question you are asking about a situation will dramatically change the outcome. For example, many years ago I was struggling to figure out how to fund an idea I had for a made-for-TV movie. The problem was that, at the time, producing a broadcast-quality television program required a lot more money than I had, and I did not know how to find funding sources.

I was stuck. I had my story treatment, a proposal, and the necessary knowledge and skills to produce the program, but I lacked the funds.

At the time, I was listening to an audio program by Brian Tracy. The audio narrator asked what we refer to in the coaching profession as a "powerful question." The question was something like, "Starting from where you are, with the resources and information you have, what action might you take to move toward your greatest goal?" Talk about a life-changing question! When I applied this to my dream of producing a video program, I immediately realized that something needed to change if I was to ever accomplish my goal.

In looking at the resources I did have, instead of the obstacles, I saw that I could accomplish my true outcome — which was and always has been to communicate ideas and information that would help people, by simply changing the medium I was planning to work in.

While I had little chance of mounting a video production, I did have the necessary skills and equipment to write and publish a book. I began writing the story immediately. While that particular story has not been and probably never will be published, writing it was the step that started me on the path to becoming a published author. This has radically altered my life and enabled me to touch the lives of more than a million people throughout the world. It has given me a life beyond anything I could have ever imagined and a personal satisfaction that goes beyond what words can describe.

All this began as a result of simply changing my original question from, "How can I find the funds?" to "With the resources and information I have, what action might I take to move toward my greatest goal?"

Activity Steps: Removing Obstacles

- What is the one obstacle standing in your way that if you were to remove it, would enable you to move toward your ultimate goal at work?
- What could you change in this situation in order to move forward?
- When will you begin?

44. *Be a Salesperson*

We are all salespeople. After all, much of our daily communication with people, whether at home or in business, is actually in the process of selling.

From the parent trying to convince (sell) their teenager to clean their room, to the young man or woman asking (selling) that special someone to go out on a date, to the employee trying to have her idea heard by the CEO, we're always engaged in the process of selling.

One of the keys to successful interpersonal communications is knowing when to make your pitch. Ask too soon, and you risk failure because the person you're trying to convince has not learned enough to make a decision. Wait too long, and you risk missing your opportunity. She's going to the prom with someone else.

Equally important is making sure you have the person's attention before you make your pitch. If your teenager is preoccupied with watching a basketball game, your strong case for his cleaning his room will go unheard. In business, if your prospective customer is busy reading email, no matter how good your presentation is, it's falling on deaf ears.

When I proposed to my wife, Georgia, I hadn't noticed that she was distracted by a waiter passing by carrying a huge lobster on a tray. Her first answer to my heartfelt proposal? "Look at the lobster!" Fortunately, she had heard enough of my proposal that when she realized I was waiting for an answer, she replied, "Yes, of course. But did you see that lobster?"

To sell your position, idea, or company, you must be able to communicate the benefits to your potential listener, but first you need to have their attention.

Farmer Ben's Donkey

A short story will illustrate my point. There were two farmers, one named Julie and the other Ben. Julie had purchased a donkey from Ben. After a few days, she brought the donkey back, complaining that it would not work. "I can't get him to do anything," she exclaimed. "He just stands there looking dumb."

Ben looked at the donkey, picked up a paddle, and hit the animal squarely across the rear, not hard enough to hurt him but enough to get his attention. The donkey's ears perked up. He stood tall and looked alert, ready to go to work.

Patiently, Ben turned to Julie and remarked, "First you have to get his attention."

While I am not suggesting that you paddle people on their rears to get their attention, I am saying that before you start telling someone what a great person you are, how your product is the best thing since sliced bread, and why she should buy from you, you must get her attention. This is critical! It is especially important if you are telemarketing to set appointments or make sales.

45. *Bounce Back*

Life happens. It doesn't matter how positive your attitude is or how balanced and centered you are; there are going to be times when you are knocked down, times when your carefully organized life is turned upside down and you get knocked on your rear end.

You will no doubt experience some type of setback. You may lose your job, you may go through a divorce, your company may move to another city, or any number of other situations may arise that will leave you feeling like you were kicked in the stomach.

Let's face it. These things happen. They're part of life, and no matter how you try to explain them away with the idea that "everything happens for a reason," they hurt. A lot! The pain begins in your heart and radiates throughout your entire being. Repeating positive phrases does not make it stop hurting.

At times like these, you're going to feel down, even depressed. You'll probably feel anger or some other manifestation of your pain. Whatever you're feeling, it's okay. It's okay to feel hurt, sad, angry. You cannot deny pain any more than you can deny fear. The only way through either of them is to give yourself permission to feel the feeling.

The question is not whether or not you will feel down; the question is how long you will stay in this disempowering state.

The difference between people who get through life's challenging moments, regardless of their gravity, and those who are immobilized by the events is what I call the "bounce factor." How quickly can you bounce back? Of course, the severity of the event will have a lot to do with the time it will take you to get past the pain and on with your life.

Let's take the example of two people being downsized from their high-tech jobs. One, whom we'll call John, is floored by the news of his dismissal. He expresses his pain by becoming angry at the company, his coworkers, and the system in general. He spends his days telling anyone who'll listen about his problem. He vents his rage on his Facebook page, an act that compounds his troubles, since employers use online public profiles to learn more about the people they're considering for employment or promotion.

As he sees it, his life is ruined, and he's blaming everyone for his troubles. People who react like John often spend weeks, months, or even years wallowing in despair until, if they're fortunate, someone close to them convinces them to seek professional help.

Mary, on the other hand, reacts much differently. Although she has gone through the same experience as John and has pretty much the same issues such as a worry about living expenses, she chooses a different response.

After a brief period of low self-esteem, self-pity, and anger, Mary decides to get back in the game. She begins contacting her network of colleagues and coworkers, avails herself of the outplacement services her former employer offered everyone, and starts actively looking for a new position. In a short time, Mary finds her dream job with an exciting new company.

While both people in our hypothetical example were laid off and both went through a period of hurting, John remained stuck in his problem, while Mary handled her loss and moved on.

This is the key. It's not whether or not life will occasionally put you into a tailspin; it's how long you remain there. When something devastating happens, allow yourself some time to grieve your loss;

however, don't allow yourself to get stuck there. Take some action. Join a support group; talk about your feelings with a trusted friend or spiritual adviser. If necessary, seek professional help.

In the case of a job loss, perhaps you'll want to take some time to reevaluate your career goals. You may even consider a career change. When you're ready, you can begin networking and making new contacts. Join LinkedIn groups in your industry. Attend social or church events. Call people you know. Do something!

One of the most important things to remember in high-stress situations is not to allow yourself to become isolated. While spending some time alone is normal, even necessary, too much isolation can be dangerous and should be avoided at all costs. Get out and be with people as soon as possible. As a friend recently reminded me, "Life is for the living." Get back to your life. In time, the pain will pass.

46. Think Like an Owner Even If You're Not One

In his wonderful book *Visionary Business*, Marc Allen, bestselling author and the publisher and owner of New World Library, wrote that one of the benefits of profit sharing was that he didn't have to worry about cutting costs throughout the company because his employees did it for him.

Since they had a vested interest in the success and profitability of the company, the employees themselves looked for ways to save money and improve the business. This idea, along with the way people are treated there, has made New World Library one of the greatest successes in the publishing industry and Marc one of the most respected people in the business.

While you may or may not receive formal profit sharing, you are being paid by your employer and being given the privilege of working there. I use the word *privilege* because that's what work is — a privilege. Your job, whatever it is, provides for you and your family. It supports your lifestyle, enables you to demonstrate your talents, and provides you (I hope) with an outlet for your creativity.

Imagine how you would feel and what your life would be like if you were not able to work. What would you do all day? What would your life be about? This may sound like the ideal life to some people but in reality it rarely is. When I was doing research for my book *Don't Let an Old Person Move into Your Body*, I observed that the older people I saw who were living active, vibrant lives were all engaged in some type of business, professional, or charitable endeavor.

And, at the other end of the age spectrum, I discovered that many young dot-com billionaires and millionaires found that after a period of doing nothing but playing they became bored and frustrated and, in most cases, returned to the business arena.

If you agree with the idea that your work is an extension of your best, creative self, then it stands to reason that you would want to be doing it. Of course, this ideal does not happen overnight, but if you follow some of the suggestions here, you can move toward it.

As someone who has been fortunate to be living his passion and purpose, I can tell you that it feels fantastic. Do I plan to ever retire? What do you think? One of my goals is to be the first hundred-year-old motivational speaker.

If you want to feel better about yourself and contribute more to your success, approach your work as if you were the owner of the company, whether or not you actually are. Pay attention to the details of your area of responsibility. When you see a way to improve a portion of your job, speak out. If you find a way to cut costs without sacrificing quality, bring it to the attention of your superiors.

Regardless of your position, you are a part of a team of people working toward a common goal, namely, to grow the company. Anything you can do to improve your specific area affects the entire business. While you may not be the owner of your company, you are the owner of your job. Take ownership of your position and be proud of what you do, regardless of your particular job at the moment.

Throughout my career I have observed two types of worker. One is what I call the "pigeons" and the other is the "eagles."

Eagles are engaged in their work. They embrace it and perform their job to the best of their ability, with joy and enthusiasm, feeling fully connected to the task at hand and the company. Eagles tend to be happy in whatever job they're performing.

Pigeons, on the other hand, just get by. They're not particularly engaged in what they do and usually can't wait to leave at the end of the day. The problem is, they're not typically very happy, nor do they usually go very far in their chosen field. They are the unhappy, disengaged people you typically see in almost every large organization.

Are you an eagle or a pigeon? Which one would you prefer to be?

47. *Promote Your Company*

I was in line at the bank one day when the teller asked the woman in front of me how she was. "Oh, I'm fine," the woman replied, "but my car is another story entirely. It keeps having problems, and I don't know if it's worth pouring more money into it or if I'd be better off just buying another one." The teller, a pleasant young woman, empathized with the woman, wished her a good day, and greeted me.

What's wrong with this scene?

Had the teller read this book or been to one of my seminars, she would have recognized the opportunity to bring her employer new business. Had she been properly trained in customer service she would have picked up on the opportunity to suggest that the woman speak with a bank officer to learn about auto loans. She may have even walked the woman over and introduced her to a bank officer.

The fact that the teller was not in sales or, as is it referred to in banking, "business development," does not mean she cannot be taught to listen to what people are saying and to recognize an opportunity to bring the bank new business when it presents itself.

Whether or not you are in sales, you can still help promote your company and, when an opportunity arises, you can seize it. You should be proud of your company and your job. If you're not, why are you spending the bulk of your waking hours working there?

Assuming you work for a company that provides quality products and services, it's only natural for you to want to tell people about them. When you're out and about, at a party or going to the mall, pay close attention to what people say to you or what they say in a group. If, for example, you're at a cocktail party and you overhear someone complaining about his shoulder pain, and you happen to work for a chiropractor, you can politely interrupt him and suggest that the doctor you work for may be able to offer some assistance with his pain. I recently did this for a friend, and he's been thanking me ever since. His chronic shoulder pain is now gone.

That's really what all sales is about. A good salesperson always pays close attention to her environment and the people around her. If during the course of her day she encounters someone with a problem or need that she and her company can help with, she will tell the person about what she does and how she can help the person meet his need or solve his problem. Some of the old sales trainers used to tell new salespeople, "Find a need and fill it."

Many companies today have branded shirts, hats, jackets, and a host of other clothing items with the company name and logo so that employees can promote and advertise the company while going about their day-to-day activities. In addition to the advertising value, these items can also be great conversation starters.

Take pride in the work you do and the company you work for. When you see an opportunity for your company to help someone you meet, talk with him about it. If possible, obtain the person's contact information and let him know that someone from your company will follow up with him. You can then turn the lead over to someone in sales or business development. It's also a good idea to stay on top of what's happening with your lead, just to make sure it's being handled. After all, you are the first point of contact for the person you're trying to help and, if you're taking ownership of your job, you'll want to ensure that the person is being treated properly.

As an added benefit to you, many organizations offer what is known as a finder's fee as a bonus for bringing in a potential new customer. Even if you do not receive a financial reward, rest assured your efforts will be recognized and rewarded in some way. Besides, you are helping the company that employs you and provides you with a way to earn a living. Regardless of the company's size, it's part of everyone's job to help grow the business whenever an opportunity to do so arises.

48. *Make Dull Tasks Fun*

In every business or job there will be times when you are required to perform a task that is, shall we say, less than wonderful. When this occurs the usual response is to moan and complain about having to perform this particular task.

Rather than complaining, why not look for ways to make the task enjoyable? When I owned an audio/video production company in New England, we had to label and pack several thousand audio CDs into several hundred individual packages and get them ready to ship. While this was not really part of my job as the program's producer, it needed to be done.

What we did, instead of complaining about it, was to find a way not only to get it done but also to have fun in the process. We organized a "packaging party," complete with beer and pizza for everyone who chipped in to help. We invited a couple of friends who were kind enough to help, and turned a boring task into a fun afternoon.

One of the people who came to help out was my business partner's college friend who was, at the time, a high-level navy scientist. Here was a man who worked on top-level defense projects, spending a Saturday assembling training programs. He had a blast. He was so happy to be doing something mundane instead of his usual highly scientific work.

There will always be boring tasks that need to be performed.

When faced with one, you have two choices. You can, like many people, start complaining about how unfair it is, how it's not really your job, and how boring it is, or you can look for ways to make it as enjoyable as possible.

It's up to you. You can choose to focus on how much you don't want to be doing this and how much you dislike it; however, all this will accomplish is to leave you feeling angry or depressed. You'll still have to complete the job at hand.

Your other choice is to find ways to make it at least bearable, if not actually fun, as we did with our packaging party. Changing your focus to find ways of making it fun will leave you feeling better and, in all likelihood, get the job finished faster.

It's your choice. You can choose to be happy, regardless of the circumstances, or you can choose to be miserable. Personally I choose happy whenever possible. The next time you're faced with a task you'd rather not do, ask yourself what you can do to make it more enjoyable.

Another way to handle these types of situations is to set up a reward for yourself for completing the task or, in the case of larger projects, for reaching a particular milestone.

Many people in sales and business are typically faced with making cold calls. I do not particularly enjoy making cold calls and have never met someone who does but sometimes it needs to be done. The way I motivate myself to do it is to establish a small reward for making a certain number of calls. I may, for instance, make an agreement with myself that I will go out for a nice lunch after completing my calls for the day.

It's not really important how you handle those undesirable tasks; however, it is important how you feel doing it. If you look for and find ways to make all aspects of your job enjoyable, you will be happier at work regardless of your assignments at the moment.

49. *Be Authentically You*

I was once in business with a man who had a habit of saying, "It's business," as a way to justify his actions. It was as if he had two different sets of values: one for his business and one for his personal life. Needless to say, our partnership didn't continue for very long.

If you want to be happier and more productive, be authentic. Don't do something in business that would not be acceptable in your personal life. Do not treat people differently at work than you do at home.

This should be obvious, but when we look around the world of commerce, it becomes clear that it's not. We see corporate executives ordering their employees to do things that are unethical and, at times, even illegal. All in the name of "business." We see companies cook the books to portray a better image to the investment community, as though it's acceptable to lie and cheat as long as it's in the best interest of the company.

Large corporations mislead consumers as well as investors, all in the name of profits. Companies that have been fined for making false claims about their products write off the fines as part of the cost of doing business. This behavior is not acceptable. It never was and it never will be.

What can you do to avoid getting caught up in these unsavory practices? For starters, make sure the company you own, work for, or want to work for is an upstanding, ethical organization. If it isn't, go elsewhere. If you are being asked to do something that goes against your beliefs, don't do it, even if it means your job.

Your integrity is all you really have to guide you. Compromise that, and you'll regret it. You may not go to jail, you may not even be found out, but the guilt you will carry around as a result of selling out will weigh you down for a very long time.

Make sure you are clear about your values (see chapter 12). Know what drives your behavior. Once you know what you stand for and what is important to you, you'll be better able to determine which actions are appropriate and which are not.

Whether at home with your family or in a negotiation for a "big deal," treat everyone you meet with caring and honesty, and you will see your success increase.

50. *Practice Gratitude*

Entire books have been written on the subject of gratitude. Rhonda Byrne, author of the enormously successful book *The Secret*, also wrote a wonderful book about gratitude entitled *The Magic*.

In his seminal book The *Science of Getting Rich*, Wallace Wattles wrote:

> It is easy to understand that the nearer we live to the source of wealth, the more wealth we shall receive; and it is easy also to understand that the soul that is always grateful lives in closer touch with God than the one which never looks to Him in thankful acknowledgment.
>
> The more gratefully we fix our minds on the Supreme when good things come to us, the more good things we will receive, and the more rapidly they will come; and the reason simply is that the attitude of gratitude draws the mind into closer touch with the source from which the blessings come.

It stands to reason, as Wattles explains, that the more we appreciate all the good we have received and all the blessings in our lives, the more good we will attract to us. This is simply the law of attraction at work. Since we attract more of whatever we focus on, putting our attention on the source of our abundance and on what we are grateful for can only attract blessings.

Regardless of your circumstances, there is always something you can be grateful for. The fact that you most likely slept in a comfortable bed last night is something to be grateful for. Many people were not so fortunate.

Considering how many people are unemployed at any given time, the fact you have a job is something else to be grateful for. If you are fortunate to be living in a free country where you can choose your job and your lifestyle, that is another reason to give thanks, not to mention all the things most of us take for granted, such as our sight, our hearing, and our physical abilities.

The fastest way I know to feel better in any situation is to focus on what you already have and can be grateful for. For whatever reason, many people look at what they don't have and on what they want while taking for granted all that they've already been given.

Studies have shown that people who make an effort to feel grateful not only feel better about their lives but are physically healthier too. Sonja Lyubomirsky, MD, author of the *The How of Happiness* and a central figure in the positive psychology world, says, "Research shows that people who are consistently grateful tend to be more helpful, more forgiving, and less materialistic than people who don't express much gratitude. Gratitude is an antidote to negative emotion, a neutralizer of envy, avarice, hostility, worry, and irritation."

When you understand the principle that everything in our world, including money, comes from our Creator, and you make a habit of steadily giving thanks for what you do have, you will begin to see more good flowing into your life.

Make a practice of saying "Thank you" when someone does something for you. It need not be a big elaborate thing. A simple thank-you will suffice.

Show your appreciation for all that you have. If you're out on a sales call and find a parking space near your prospective client's office, take a moment and acknowledge your appreciation. As a matter of fact, if you ask for a parking space before you leave home, if you expect it to be there, and if you show your appreciation, you will find that you always seem to have a space to park.

If you have food to eat, give thanks for all that was involved in bringing it to your table.

Activity Step: Practice Gratitude

If you'd like to see more money flowing into your life, each night before bed make a list of five to ten things from your day that you are grateful for. They may be something as simple as someone buying you a cup of coffee at work or your coworker finishing a project for you simply because she saw you were overwhelmed and wanted to help.

I realize this may seem like a strange suggestion, especially if you have not been exposed to these ideas before, but just give it a try. I can almost guarantee that, if you complete this simple gratitude exercise each day for the next thirty days, you will see an increase in your finances. I can't explain why this works, but I know from experience that it does.

51. *Let Your Feelings Be the Guide*

A number of years ago I had the distinct pleasure of being part of a coach training program with a group of top coaches from around the globe. We were studying a specific coaching system that was based on the law of attraction and was designed to produce quantum growth for our business clients.

If you've studied personal development you've no doubt heard the idea that our feelings about a particular thing, rather than our thoughts, are the real power behind the law of attraction, that we attract what we focus on. Unfortunately most of us have been taught to "think through" our ideas and actions instead of to feel through them.

As a result of this training, with a group that was made up of mainly women, I saw my language change. I'll admit, it was pretty strange at first. Like most men, I was used to using words that described how I thought about something. The women, on the other hand, would say things like "icky" or "dark" to describe how they felt about an unpleasant idea, or if they felt good about the idea, they might say "juicy" when asked about it.

I guarantee you that if I ask one of my male friends how they feel about a particular situation they may say, "It stinks," or, "It's lousy," but they will not say, "It feels icky to me." As strange as it seemed at first, I soon found myself using similar words to describe how I felt about a particular plan and whether the thought of doing it felt exciting or "heavy."

Our emotions are our built-in guidance system. They clearly indicate whether something is in alignment with our true selves, with who we really are. If the thought of doing something feels good, it is in alignment with us. If it feels "icky," it is not.

Our emotional guidance system lets us know, at any given moment, whether we are in alignment with our desires, fully connected to our higher selves, attracting what we want. If we feel good, we are aligned. If we feel bad, then we know our thoughts are not serving us. That's why thinking them leaves us feeling down.

Knowing whether or not you are in alignment with what you desire is simply a matter of paying attention to how you feel. Your job is to monitor your feelings. When whatever you're thinking about or focusing on causes you to feel good, you're in alignment with attracting what you desire.

If you're feeling an unpleasant emotion like anger, greed, envy, or fear, or any other emotion that is not serving you, it simply means that you are focusing on something other than what you desire.

If you want to feel better and thus attract to you what you want, all you need to do is reach for a thought that feels even a tiny bit better. As you continue to do this, always going toward a more positive thought, you will be moving up the emotional scale.

By continuing to focus on what you want and what you are grateful for and to monitor how you feel, you will move more and more into alignment with the energy of what you want. You will be working with the power of the law of attraction, instead of working against it, which is what many people habitually do.

Too many people spend their time and energy thinking and speaking about all the things they don't want and everything that's wrong with their life. Because this kind of griping is out of alignment with who they really are, it leaves them feeling lousy and, by virtue of the laws of the Universe, keeps attracting the same conditions over and over.

If you want to change what's showing up in your life you must change what you are telling yourself over and over. You need to stop giving attention to what you do not want and start seeing what you do.

You can literally change the story you have been telling yourself about "how things are." There is no "how things are." What you are attracting into your life — the good, the not-so-good, and everything in between — is the result of what you have been telling yourself and focusing on.

Remember that what you envision your life to be is accepted by your subconscious mind as being true whether or not it actually is at this moment. Your subconscious does not distinguish between what you vividly imagine and what is real. It simply responds to your every desire, which it receives through your thoughts, words, emotions, and actions.

It is quite true that the most important thing you can do, as Esther Hicks says in her law of attraction seminars, "is to feel good."

If you feel good you are in alignment with universal forces and are attracting your desires to you. If you feel less than good, you are not.

52. *Listen to Music*

I n his megahit song "Sir Duke" from the *Songs in the Key of Life* album, music legend Stevie Wonder wrote about how music is a world within itself and how it celebrates life.

Yes, music is a world within itself. And as a memory trigger, music is second only to our sense of smell. Listening to a piece of music can have an immediate effect on how you feel in the moment, particularly if the song brings back happy memories.

You'll be driving along in your car, listening to the radio, and you hear a song that immediately transports you to a past event. It may be the song that you and your special someone were listening to when you met. You can see the entire scene vividly, even though the event took place years or even decades ago. This happens because the brain has linked these two events, the song and the occasion. This is known as the Hebbian learning rule, which states, "Neurons that fire together, wire together."

Music as a Feel-Good Tool

Aside from helping you to retrieve pleasant memories from the past, music can also improve how you feel at work or in any other situation. Suppose you have been asked to give a presentation in front of your company's top management. While this presents an opportunity for you to shine, it is also more than a little intimidating. Perhaps, like many people, you're uncomfortable speaking in front of large groups.

Of course, you'll be well prepared. You may even have joined Toastmasters, a global organization that helps people overcome their fear of public speaking and learn to be more comfortable in front of an audience. (If you do wish to become a better public speaker or simply become more at ease speaking before an audience, I highly recommend attending Toastmasters. It's one of the best things you can do for your professional development.)

On top of becoming as well prepared as possible and devoting time to rehearsing your presentation, you can use music to give you a boost of energy and enthusiasm before your speech. Put together a playlist of some of the songs that trigger good feelings and that make you feel strong and powerful.

On my own feel-good playlist I have the theme from the movie *Rocky*, James Brown's "I Got You (I Feel Good)," and Billy Joel's "We Didn't Start the Fire" because that was the song that was playing when I did the firewalk with Tony Robbins years ago. That song is anchored in my mind to feelings of absolute power and peak energy. Listening to it and the other songs on my playlist immediately raises my energy and puts me in a powerful state of mind.

You may remember watching the Olympics when swimmer Michael Phelps was about to break the record for winning the most medals. Just before his events he could be seen plugging in his iPod. Listening to his personal playlist was part of his ritual for getting ready for the biggest event of his life.

You can use this same strategy in any area of your life. In addition to playing a feel-good song list before making a presentation, you can use music to invoke a variety of mental states.

If you're writing an important report or a white paper, you can use music that will calm you and spark your creativity. Or you could choose music that produces specific brainwaves to invoke a desirable mental state. This is accomplished by mixing various frequencies to "trick" your brain into mental states such as meditation, creativity, and even healing. The best known sources for these types of programs are the Monroe Institute (www.monroeinstitute.org) and Sounds True (www.soundstrue.com).

You can use music to improve how you feel and to increase your productivity at any time.

53. *See the Big Picture*

There's an old story about a group of men working as welders on an assembly line, making parts for a spaceship. When a visitor asked one of the men what he was doing, the man grumbled, "I'm assembling these metal parts," and continued with his work, doing what he was told, nothing more, nothing less, until quitting time.

The next man, who also seemed pretty unhappy, mumbled something about being a welder and continued on with his work. Both men seemed to be your typical disgruntled factory workers, drudging through their day, counting the minutes until quitting time.

As he approached the third man, the visitor could not help but notice that this man was humming a tune to himself and appeared quite happy. Surprised by this, especially after encountering the two unhappy men, the visitor became curious to know why this particular man seemed happier than the others.

When he approached the man and asked what he was doing, the man stood tall and proudly declared, "I'm welding these parts for a critical assembly in the spaceship that will be taking men into space and bringing them safely back home. I'm proud to be doing such important work."

What was it that made the one man happy and satisfied in his work while the others were, like far too many people, quite unhappy and for all practical purposes disengaged from their jobs?

You've probably figured out by now that the man who was proud, satisfied, and happy in his work was connected to his job and saw the bigger picture. He recognized that he was playing a part in launching men and women into space and getting them safely back home, while the others saw only their small task.

Being engaged with and connected to your work is an important component of a happy and productive life. Regardless of how unimportant your job may appear, if you examine it closely I think you'll find that, in most cases, what you're doing is part of a bigger, more important outcome. When you put your job in this perspective, you are more likely to feel better about yourself and your role at work.

Whether you're a senior vice president, an account executive, a stock room clerk, or a janitor, you have a purpose and play a part in the overall success of the business.

Whenever I'm in a public restroom that is clean and well maintained, I make a point of thanking the people who are responsible. I love the look on their faces when they realize that I'm complimenting their work, not making a complaint. This is something that costs me nothing to do, takes only a minute or two, and helps someone feel better about themselves and their job.

By the way, a simple thank-you will often be the one thing that makes someone's day. We all need to be acknowledged for who we are and what we're doing. It's also an ideal way to handle compliments. There's no need to get all gushy when someone says something nice about you or compliments you on a new outfit. More important, don't just brush it off by saying, "It's no big deal," or, "It's an old dress." All this does is lower your own self-esteem. Just calmly say, "Thank you," and move on.

54. Develop Meaningful Friendships at Work

Depending on the size of the company you work for, your job can provide you with the opportunity to develop meaningful friendships. As a matter of fact, a high percentage of married couples met at work, and numerous lifelong friendships began in the workplace.

A word of caution here. Being in a romantic relationship with a coworker can be a recipe for disaster — not to mention that in many workplaces fraternizing among employees is a violation of company policy and may be cause for dismissal, so proceed carefully. While your place of employment, especially if it's a very large company, can be a great place to meet your special someone, it can also create problems if things don't work out. Seeing someone daily with whom you were involved and having to work with him or her can be awkward, so you may want to think twice before getting involved at work. Of course, the larger the company, the less problematic romantic entanglements at work are.

Romance aside, your workplace is an ideal environment for developing lasting friendships. You have an opportunity to meet people and get to know them in a nonthreatening setting. Because you work together, you already have common ground on which to build. And you will encounter people with whom you share common interests. Socializing with these people is a natural outgrowth of your common interests.

In many organizations there are even formal associations of retired employees. For example, retirees from the Bell Telephone companies can join the Telephone Pioneers of America, a national association that provides a way for people to remain connected to one another and to the industry in general. They produce a newsletter, offer member benefits, and hold regular gatherings for former Bell employees to meet up in person.

If you work for a large organization you'll likely have a variety of opportunities to partake in activities ranging from softball and bowling to Weight Watchers and other support meetings, organized by someone within the company. Even in smaller companies there are usually afterwork activities that allow you to get to know and befriend your colleagues.

If you take the time to get to know your fellow workers on a personal level, you'll find that work becomes more pleasant, and you will most likely be more productive. It's easier to work with people you've had an opportunity to get to know on a personal level.

55. *State Your Intentions*

When there's something that you want to have or to accomplish, do you, like many people, sit around and wait for it but don't think you'll ever get it? Most people wish for something — be it a promotion at work, an increase in their salary, or simply more money — but do not really expect to receive it. And when they don't, they simply write it off as "just the way things are."

If you've been living this way, now is the time to stop. Now is the time to start using your God-given power and live your life on purpose. Now is the time to start "intending" what you want your life to become.

Several years ago I was introduced to the concept of intending in the book *The Intenders Handbook* by Tony Burroughs and invited by a friend to take part in a group she was starting.

Our group, which consisted of five or six people, met at a friend's home. After settling in, socializing, and sharing some snacks, one by one we would recite aloud our intentions, beginning with the phrase, "I intend that...," followed by whatever we wanted at the time, and ending with the phrase "for the highest and best good for all."

One of the members of our group was the eleven-year-old daughter of our host. One of her intentions was to be a journalism major at Syracuse University. It's been more than a decade since our group met, and I had not seen our host, Pat, for several years until I ran into her at a business event recently. When I asked how her daughter was doing, Pat replied, "Oh, she's doing great. She's at Syracuse University, majoring in journalism." She then reminded me that doing so was one of the intentions her daughter used to state at our weekly meetings back when she was just a child.

If you want to learn how you can join an existing group, either in person or online, or obtain *The Intenders Handbook* or start your own group, visit www.intenders.com.

Whether or not you pursue a formal group, invoking the power of the word *intention* instead of simply hoping or wishing will increase the probability of your success. Words are powerful and, obviously, some words are more powerful than others. The word *intend* is one of the more powerful verbs you can use.

Beginning your affirmative statement with the words *I intend* is a powerful way to declare your heartfelt desires to the Universe.

Don't fall into the trap of wishing and hoping your dreams come true and then saying, "Oh, well" and staying stuck where you are. You are bigger than that. You have within you the power to change your life, in any way, at any time.

As Marianne Williamson wrote in her wonderful book *A Return to Love*, "Your playing small serves no one."

56. *Avoid Energy Zappers*

Every company has them. Energy zappers are those people who spend their days telling whomever will listen all about their latest illnesses or the accident that happened on the freeway. These are the people whose mission in life is to make everyone feel as bad as they do.

They're negative people who seem obsessed with finding something wrong in every situation. If it's a beautiful, sunny day they'll tell you about the storm that's coming tomorrow. They lie in wait for some terrible tragedy to befall them instead of enjoying the present moment.

While they may be good, caring people, they're difficult to be around. If you're having a fantastic day the energy zapper will come along and rain on your parade. You know the people I'm referring to. We all have them in our lives. Unfortunately, many times they're some of the people who are closest to us, perhaps even family members. You may be going along having a fantastic day, feeling awesome, as happy as can be, when suddenly you encounter the energy zapper. Within five minutes of listening to her, you feel like you need a nap. She sucks the energy and good feelings out of you.

The best thing you can do with these people is to spend as little time around them as possible. Obviously if they're in your family you can't avoid them altogether, but you can minimize the time you spend with them. If they're at your workplace you can do your best to avoid them or at least not get caught up in their story.

Trying to change an energy zapper, unless he wants to change, is usually a waste of time. My mother-in-law, Jean, used to make a game out of it. Someone would say something like, "Isn't it a lovely day?" to which she would reply, "It's too hot," "It's too cold," or too something. The person would then try to convince her that it was, in fact, a beautiful day. At that point, as Sherlock Holmes would have said, "The game's afoot." Jean would continue to defend her position, countering any attempt to make her feel better. I was one of the few people who'd interrupt her game by refusing to get caught up in it.

Her classic remark, as she got older was, "It's not easy getting old." This statement was designed to get someone to try to make her feel better. Having spent so much time in self-discovery and self-reflection I had learned better ways to communicate and to avoid getting sucked into people's games. My standard reply each time she said that was, "The alternative is even worse," at which point she'd smile, realizing I'd caught her at her game. I think one of the reasons she liked me so much was the fact that she couldn't manipulate me like she could everyone else, especially her husband and daughter.

In your workplace you know who the energy zappers are. The best thing you can do is spend as little time around them as possible. As they say in 12-step programs, "Hang out with the winners."

If you want to be happier and more productive at work and enjoy your life to its fullest, spend time with the winners, those people who are positive, uplifting, and supportive and who want to help you become the best you can be.

57. Take Charge of Your Emotions

How many times have we all said things like, "So-and-so makes me angry," or, "When this or that happens it makes me mad"?

Are these statements true?

I'd like you to try a little experiment. First, think about the worst day you've ever had at work. Perhaps it was the day your boss embarrassed you in front of the group. Maybe it was the day you make a huge mistake, costing the company a small fortune. Recall what happened, who was there, what was said, and all the details you can. In your mind, put yourself back in the scene, feeling and experiencing it as though it were actually happening.

Now how do you feel?

I'm going to guess you feel pretty lousy recalling this day you would just as soon forget.

Next, I'd like you to recall your best, most amazing day. What was that like? What were you doing? Replay this scene in your mind, feeling and experiencing it in as much detail as you can. Hear the sounds that were there in the moment; smell the smells. Really immerse yourself in the feelings you had on that fantastic day.

Now how do you feel?

This time I'm going to take a wild guess and say you feel pretty amazing or at least really, really good.

Okay. What did we just learn?

You were able to switch from feeling poorly, maybe even depressed, to feeling great. You did all this with your thoughts or, more accurately, with what you were telling yourself. The scenes were not actually taking place, and there was no one there to affect how you felt.

If you ask people why they are not happier you will typically hear a litany of reasons that, most likely, involve blaming people and circumstances for how they feel when, in reality, how they feel is totally within their control.

You choose how you feel in response to whatever is taking place around you. At any time you can choose to feel better simply by changing what you're focused on in the moment.

This is one of the reasons I suggest you limit the amount of news you watch and if you must watch or read the news, try not to become emotionally invested in it. Overidentifying with stories in the news will cause you to change your emotional state as quickly as you just did in the exercise above. Understand that it is you and your emotional response to what you're watching or reading that is creating your unhappiness.

The good news is that you can change it in a moment simply by changing what you place your attention on. If you read stories of people who have endured horrors and managed to come through emotionally intact, you will find that they devised ways to reframe their circumstances. They internally represented what was happening in a different way than those who did not fare as well. In effect, they took charge of their internal communication and, thus, their emotions.

There it is! When you learn to take charge of your thoughts, which determine how you feel, you become master of your mind and are able to choose how you respond in any circumstance.

When you find yourself going into a negative spiral, stop your train of thought. Just interrupt your thinking and ask, "What thought could I think, right now, that would feel just a little bit better than what I'm thinking?" If need be, reframe the situation by asking something like, "What's good about this?" Little by little you will begin to feel better as you change your focus and raise your emotional state.

58. *Remember That Money Is a Measure of Your Service*

I remember it as if it happened last week, though it has been more than thirty years since I was in the audience at a network marketing rally in Las Vegas. One of the company leaders, a well-dressed, attractive woman, walked to the podium to speak. Her opening remark, something that was to become almost like a mantra for me, was, "Money is a measure of your service. If you want more money, provide more service."

That phrase has served me well ever since her words first echoed across the crowded hotel ballroom. It's a simple concept, right? Why, then, do so many people complain that they do not earn enough money? Why do so many people in the workplace feel that they should be paid more simply because they show up each day for work? We have come to expect cost of living increases in our salary each year, whether or not we've actually done anything to warrant a raise.

As a matter of fact, if you cannot see how you have directly contributed to your company's bottom line, you may want to start looking for work somewhere else. Just getting by in business is no longer acceptable. Companies are ferreting out unproductive employees and replacing them with people who are engaged in their work and want to do a good job.

If you want to earn more money, simply find ways to render

more service to your employer. In our society people are paid based on three things: the demand for what they do, the skills and education required to perform the work, and how easily they can be replaced.

People who are at the lower end of the pay scale are typically paid minimum wage or slightly more because their job does not require a lot of training, there is not a big demand for their limited skills, and they are easily replaced.

On the other hand, people at the top of the pay scale earn many times what those at the bottom earn because their job requires a lot of training and knowledge, there is a high demand for their skills, and they are difficult to replace.

If you want to earn more money, find ways to become more valuable to your employer. Doing so may require you to go back to school or in some other way to increase your value to the company. Acquiring specialized knowledge will raise your level of expertise and make you more difficult to replace.

Another way you can become of greater value to your company, and as a result earn more money, is to find ways to add more value to the organization.

A number of years ago my friend Wayne Nicholson was employed by a college to manage an adult-learning program for disabled people. Being of an entrepreneurial mind-set, and seeing an unmet need for these people to learn how to live independently, he created an Independent Living program and proposed it to the college. Being a pretty smart guy, he designed it in such a way that it would be inexpensive for the college to implement. Wayne proposed that, in lieu of a pay raise, he would receive a percentage of the added revenue to the school.

As it turned out, the program was an enormous success and Wayne received a significant increase in his income. By removing any financial risk on the part of the college he was able to get his proposal accepted and, as a result, earned more money both for himself and for the school.

Many larger companies have instituted what has become known as an "Intrapreneur" program. This is a program in which an individual working in the organization "takes direct responsibility for turning an idea into a profitable finished product through assertive risk taking and innovation," as *The American Heritage Dictionary* defines it. The term is attributed to management consultant Gifford Pinchot, author of the book *Intrapreneuring in Action*.

If, like me, you've always leaned toward entrepreneurial endeavors, Intrapreneurship may be one way you can grow your income while remaining with your present company.

Activity Steps: Adding Value

- What are some ways in which you can become more valuable to your employer?
- Is there a way, within your area of responsibility, that you can save the company money? Many companies offer financial and other rewards for cost-cutting ideas they implement.

59. *Live in the Present*

I f you listen carefully to what people say, you will quickly realize that many of them spend most of their waking hours living in the past or future. They talk about how wonderful life was way back when, in some long-ago time. They reminisce about the "good old days" and how they wish things were that way again. The truth is, the good old days were not all that good. We just remember them as being that way because our mind typically retains the good from the past but not the rest. Reflecting on and reminiscing about the past is not necessarily a bad thing, but trying to live there is absurd.

When they're not yearning for the past, people live in some far-off imaginary future — all the while missing out on the present, which is the only time that exists.

Life is taking place in the here and now.

Now is the only time that exists. It is also where your personal power lies. Louise Hay, author of several books and the founder of Hay House, one of the leading metaphysical and personal-development publishing companies, wrote in *You Can Heal Your Life*, "The point of power is in the present moment."

This is a significant statement. Now is where you work, live your life, and create your future. What you are feeling in the present moment is what is attracting your future circumstances to you. At work, the job you're doing today is paving the way for your future success, or lack thereof. This is another reason to always deliver your best.

Living in the now is the way to feel at ease and protected. We experience stress when our mind is focused on a past or future event. We become upset when we replay a past mistake or worry about a nonexistent future. The truth is, there is no worry in the present.

This idea has been written about for centuries, from the Bible message of "Watch ye therefore: for you know not when the Master comes" (Mark 13:35), to author Baba Ram Dass's classic *Remember: Be Here Now*, to *The Power of Now* by Eckhart Tolle, which advises us, "Realize deeply that the present moment is all you have. Make the now the primary focus of your life."

The more you can remain in the present, the more your life will flow. Ideas will come to you. The solution to a pressing problem will pop into your mind, and your stress will lessen or disappear altogether.

Does this mean you should not imagine your ideal future? Of course not, but it's important to realize that while you're envisioning your magnificent future, you are doing so in the present time. There's nothing wrong with building castles in the sky as long as you don't try to move into them.

What really matters is how you are feeling right now. Since you are, by virtue of the law of attraction, creating and attracting your future based on how you feel in the present, it is essential to do whatever you can to feel good now.

If you find yourself in a stressful situation, or feeling worried or fearful, stop whatever you are doing and become still for a moment or two. Take a couple of long, slow, deep breaths. As you exhale, feel yourself connecting to the earth. Continue to do this, if only for a minute or two, and you will begin to feel calmer. As you become more centered, your mind will quiet and you will be able to access more of your personal power. You may even want to imagine a bright light of protection from the heavens. Allow this light to engulf you, and let yourself feel its divine power.

The more you practice living in the present, the more your life will be in flow. If you want to know more about this idea, I suggest you read Tolle's *The Power of Now*.

60. *Get Up and Start Moving*

It's not going to be a surprise to anyone when I say that people, especially in the United States, are terribly out of shape. The obesity problem in the States has reached a critical level and is costing billions of dollars in added health-care costs. We are among the unhealthiest people in the world, raking thirty-third on the list of the world's healthiest countries (United Nations, World Bank, World Health Organization, 2012). We consume more food and have higher health-care costs than any other country. The problem has even moved into the adolescent population, creating a situation that could, if not addressed and rectified, bankrupt our health-care system.

One suggestion, made to me by the owner of my local health club, is to simply get up and start moving. We have become such a sedentary society, with all our modern conveniences. With so many people using computers while sitting at their desks, it's no wonder we're out of shape. A few generations ago there were no health clubs or fitness centers. People worked at jobs that required physical activity beyond clicking a mouse. Today, unless you live in a big city, where people walk places, you most likely drive to a job that requires little or no physical activity.

It's very easy to slip into a lifestyle with little physical activity.

I know, I have a tendency to do so too. For me, it takes making and keeping a commitment to ensure I am taking care of my health.

What about you? Are you physically active, ensuring you get enough exercise to keep in shape, or are you part of the couch potato crowd? If you want to lead a full, active, and productive life, you need to take care of your body. Achieving any level of success requires physical energy. Too many people climbing the ladder of success run out of steam halfway there due to their poor health.

Regardless of your current physical condition there are steps you can take to start regaining your health and fitness.

Some simple steps to get started include things like parking farther away from your building so you have a little longer walk to and from your workplace, using stairs instead of elevators, walking across your office to speak with a colleague rather than texting or calling, and taking a walk during your lunch hour. You may even want to create a small walking group with some coworkers to make it easier to stay motivated. If you want to try something really different, holding meetings with another person while walking can be highly productive, especially if you do it somewhere serene. I've held many one-on-one meetings walking along the Delaware Canal. The peaceful backdrop and natural setting spark new ideas.

One of our problems as a society is our addiction to instant gratification. We are accustomed to having whatever we want as soon as we want it.

While this rarely works in most instances, it never works when it comes to physical health. Losing weight and becoming physically fit takes time. If you're overweight and out of shape and want to do something about it, create a long-range plan, complete with goals and an action plan. As you would with any change in diet or physical activity, talk with your health-care practitioner before you begin.

Several years ago I was at an unhealthy weight. I felt lousy and didn't like the way I looked. I made a commitment to myself to do something about it. Wanting to model success, I joined Weight Watchers, since they have a long track record of helping people lose weight and keep it off. When I first joined I calculated how much weight I wanted to lose. Estimating a weight loss of about a pound a week, an amount that the body can handle without going into famine mode, I paid in advance for the number of weeks I'd need to reach my goal.

This gave me a financial commitment as well as a mental one. It never hurts to invest some money to gain extra motivation. I had my commitment, my goal, and the date I expected to reach it. I was ready. All I needed to do was follow a simple program that had worked for millions of people before me. I started following the dietary changes suggested by the program and began a regular exercise program. I reached my goal two weeks before my date and felt great. That was more than a decade ago and, while my weight has varied somewhat over the years, I have never approached the weight I started from.

If you're ready to change your habits and become healthier, commit now to begin making better food choices and to start exercising.

As any health coach will tell you, you don't have to try to run a marathon; you just need to start moving.

Conclusion

Congratulations! As a result of having read this book you have taken a major step toward taking charge of your success and creating the life you were born to live.

If you skipped over any chapters or have not completed all the Activity Steps, please go back and complete them now. These simple activities will make a huge difference in your life.

You now have a toolbox of ideas and techniques you can use, at any time, to improve how you feel and to mold a life that is more enjoyable, happier, and more amazing than you ever thought possible.

How do I know this? As you read in the pages of this book, I have been using these exact principles in my own life for more than twenty-five years. I have watched, sometimes in awe, as my life has kept getting better and more interesting. It continues to do so to this day.

Of course, there are times in everyone's life when things are going less than great. During those times, pick this book back up and reread the chapters that pertain to whatever challenge you are experiencing.

As you read in chapter 34 about reading personal development regularly, you'll want to continue your journey of discovery. Continuing to make small incremental improvements in each area of your life will enable you to lead a life beyond anything you've ever expected.

Make a lifelong commitment to reading, watching, and listening to uplifting, life-affirming ideas and information. Just five or ten minutes a day will have a profound effect on your success. When you're at the gym working out, invest in your own success by listening to audio programs or reading a self-help or business book, rather than watching some mindless TV show that just happens to be on the screen in front of you.

The payback for your small time-investment to learn about ways to improve your circumstances is having the life you've always wanted. And the reason it's important to do it on a regular, ideally daily, basis is that we all get off track from time to time. A steady diet of positive ideas will help you stay on track.

Be sure to subscribe to my *Jim's Jems* ezine in order to continue your study. You will, from time to time, receive gifts from me, as well as learn about new programs that may interest you. I promise not to overwhelm you with email, and I will never share your information with anyone, period.

I wish you the very best of success in your career and your life. If at any time I can be of assistance, please let me know. I encourage you to connect with me on Facebook or LinkedIn, to follow me on Twitter, or to subscribe to my YouTube channel.

God bless you.

— Jim Donovan
Bucks County, Pennsylvania

About the Author

J im Donovan, who for eighteen years has been a speaker and a coach, is a recognized thought leader in the field of personal development. In addition, his books and teachings have positively impacted the lives of millions of people throughout the world.

Speaking openly about his pain and struggle, what he calls his "decade of destruction," and sharing the ideas and techniques that enabled him to radically change his life have made him a sought-after speaker and trainer for business events and meetings. Jim's unique sense of humor, coupled with his varied life experiences, allows him to connect with people from all walks of life.

Several of his books have been international bestsellers, bringing his message of hope and possibility to people everywhere. Jim's articles have appeared in numerous print and digital magazines, and he is a frequent media guest and expert source on human performance and personal development.

His *Jim's Jems* ezine has been published online since 1992. A free subscription and complimentary gift are available at his website, www.JimDonovan.com.

Jim, a native New Yorker, now enjoys what he considers the best of all worlds, living with his wife, Georgia, their cats, and myriad wild animals in a beautiful, wooded area of upper Bucks County, Pennsylvania, just north of Philadelphia and an hour and a half from New York City.

NEW WORLD LIBRARY is dedicated to publishing books and other media that inspire and challenge us to improve the quality of our lives and the world.

We are a socially and environmentally aware company, and we strive to embody the ideals presented in our publications. We recognize that we have an ethical responsibility to our customers, our staff members, and our planet.

We serve our customers by creating the finest publications possible on personal growth, creativity, spirituality, wellness, and other areas of emerging importance. We serve New World Library employees with generous benefits, significant profit sharing, and constant encouragement to pursue their most expansive dreams.

As a member of the Green Press Initiative, we print an increasing number of books with soy-based ink on 100 percent postconsumer-waste recycled paper. Also, we power our offices with solar energy and contribute to nonprofit organizations working to make the world a better place for us all.

Our products are available
in bookstores everywhere.
For our catalog, please contact:

New World Library
14 Pamaron Way
Novato, California 94949

Phone: 415-884-2100 or 800-972-6657
Catalog requests: Ext. 50
Orders: Ext. 10
Fax: 415-884-2199
Email: escort@newworldlibrary.com

To subscribe to our electronic newsletter, visit:
www.newworldlibrary.com